D0915554

Golden Cloud, Silver Lining
LESSONS FROM THE MASTERS
ON HAPPINESS
& LONGEVITY

Golden Cloud, Silver Lining

LESSONS FROM THE MASTERS
on HAPPINESS
& LONGEVITY

The Dalai Lama
Deepak Chopra
Wayne W. Dyer
The Karmapa
Sri Sri Ravi Shankar
The Kenting Tai Situpa
Rohini Singh
Robert Holden
Khushwant Singh
Shobhaa Dé

EDITED BY
ASHOK CHOPRA

HAY HOUSE INDIA
Australia • Canada • Hong Kong • India
South Africa • United Kingdom • United States

Hay House Publishers (India) Pvt. Ltd.
Muskaan Complex, Plot No.3, B-2 Vasant Kunj, New Delhi-110 070, India
Hay House Inc., PO Box 5100, Carlsbad, CA 92018-5100, USA
Hay House UK, Ltd., 292-B Kensal Rd., London W10 5BE, UK
Hay House Australia Pty Ltd., 18/36 Ralph St., Alexandria NSW 2015, Australia
Hay House SA (Pty) Ltd., PO Box 990, Witkoppen 2068, South Africa
Hay House Publishing, Ltd., 17/F, One Hysan Ave., Causeway Bay, Hong Kong
Raincoast, 9050 Shaughnessy St., Vancouver, BC V6P 6E5, Canada

Email: contact@hayhouse.co.in
www.hayhouse.co.in

ISBN 978-93-81431-52-8

Designed and typeset at
Hay House India

Printed at Thomson Press (India) Ltd., Faridabad, Haryana (India)

to
om arora
my habib, my hafeez, my rehnuma

Khushian hazar hain dil-e-muztar liye huey
Qatra hai bayqarar sumundar liye huey

– Asghar Gondvi

(The restless heart is brimming with thousands of joys
Like a single drop carries a stormy ocean in it)

Contents

INTRODUCTION

ashok chopra

NOT BY BREAD ALONE

This above all: to thine own self be true.

– William Shakespeare: *Hamlet*

IT ISN'T SURPRISING THAT AS THE WORLD ECONOMY goes into a downturn and austerity is touted as the panacea for all the ills of profligacy, 'the happiness industry' has been taken over by economists if only to make us forget the hard times that lie ahead and to make recommendations to governments on how best to cushion us from the knocks to come. The industry isn't concerned either with Jean-Jacques Rousseau's (the guru of happiness) belief that contentment is 'nothing external to ourselves and our own existence' or with, as one of the fundamental tenets of Buddhism puts it, 'happiness is not the realization of one's desires but coming to terms with our inner selves'.

This industry is now big time having achieved an early pinnacle of success with the publication of the First World Happiness Report in April 2012. It was commissioned by a UN Conference on Happiness under the auspices of the UN General Assembly edited by two happiness experts: Richard Layard of the London School of Economics and John Helliwell of the University of British Columbia. Details are provided at the website (www. World Happiness Report) but the summing up was done by a group of experts, including Daniel Kahneman who won the Nobel Prize in economics (2002) and is author of the bestseller, *Thinking, Fast and Slow* (published in 2011).

Before getting into the Western concepts of what constitutes happiness, a little background on what led to the present interest in happiness apart from the economic crisis that has hit everyone in the West and is now spreading to the eastern hemisphere as well. Harvard researchers have segregated people's feelings into 'effective happiness' (every-day ups and downs) and 'evaluative happiness' (a person's overall assessment of his or her own life).

Indicators that look at happiness from different points of view have been created. For instance, two Harvard psychologists have used iPhone apps to ask volunteers questions like: 'How happy were you yesterday?'; or 'All things considered how satisfied are you with your own life as a whole nowadays?'; or 'Taking all things together would you say you are very happy, quite happy, not very happy, or not at all happy?'

These questions are too glib and take us nowhere. It isn't surprising then that different answers give economists plenty to argue about. That may well be a dead end, argue economists but the exercise is still worth it because happiness can be measured objectively: happiness has predictable causes and is correlated to specific entities such as health, wealth, income, status and power. Therefore they argue it should be possible for governments to create the right conditions for happiness to flourish. Economists want governments as guides to public policy rather like they use the gross national product (GNP) to do so.

But this approach begs the question: can GNP be used to determine happiness or is it up to the individual how best to pursue it? After all, likes and dislikes vary considerably and what may make one individual happy may not have the same effect on another. Happiness is therefore a matter to be pursued individually. Governments meddling with happiness only confuses issues. Clearly, earlier classics – such as Yevgeny Zamyatin's 1921-published dystopian novel *We*, Aldous Huxley's *Brave New World* (1932), George Orwell's *Animal Farm* (1945) and *1984* (1949) and several others – need to be checked out again.

The more closely you follow the Happiness World and the Western debates around it, it appears that happiness gurus are tinkering at the edges when profound understanding is required. Without going into the realm of philosophy, it may be appropriate to quote a couple of Western thinkers:

> Bertrand Russell: Happiness is a deep instinctive union with the stream of life.

> Albert Einstein: The most incomprehensible thing about the universe is that it is comprehensible.

Plus, we have the wisdom of saints and sages down the ages in sayings such as 'know thyself' or 'the Kingdom of God is inside you'.

In other words, what they have said is that we need to understand the universe we live in and learn to live within its rules. But the catch is: What are these rules and how do we observe them? We don't really know the external world; we know it only through our senses but clearly there is no reliable guide. So, all we can do as individuals is to understand ourselves for which our own body and mind are the laboratory. 'It is all there in the mind', as the cliché goes.

***

When you look at the Western debates on the meaning of happiness, there is just one conclusion that can be reached: Happiness can't be achieved by bread alone. We need to seek various other sources such as art, literature, poetry, music, cinema and scriptures, both Western and

Eastern, to arrive at some working definition of the key constituents of the happiness package.

Here are some words of wisdom from the sages/sacred texts of both the West and the East, which could be taken as a guide to action:

Words do not the saint or sinner make
Action alone is written in the book of fate,
What we sow that alone we take.

Guru Nanak

People of the Book,
do not go to excess in your religion.

The Quran

Go to the ant, thou sluggard; consider her ways,
    and be wise;
Which having no guide, overseer, or ruler, Provideth
her meat in the summer, and gathereth her food in
    the harvest.

The Bible, Proverbs

Don't be boastful. Don't be short-tempered. Don't make a short-lived attempt. Don't expect gratitude.

The Dalai Lama

Train your eyes and ears; train your nose and tongue. The senses are good friends when they are trained. Train your body in deeds, train your tongue in words, train your mind in thoughts. This training will take you beyond sorrow.

Meditate, meditate. Do not run after sense pleasures. Do not swallow a red-hot iron ball and then cry 'I am in great pain'.

The Dhammapada

Unlike the Hindu tradition, which the Buddha sought to change, the spiritual elite he sought to create owed nothing to family background or heredity. According to the Buddha, an individual's caste 'is due solely to his success in freeing from selfish desire. This high state also shows itself in a patience which is like an army, holding up against blows, verbal abuse, or any other attack. The elite has crossed the torrential river of craving once and for all. But always bear in mind not to give your attention to what others do or fail to do; give it to what you do or fail to do'.

The great Indian epic, the Mahabharata – an account of a war (and all the events that led to it) between cousins (the Pandavas on one side and the Kauravas on the other) – is not a religious work in the strict sense of the term. It is a call to action; it depicts a state of complete detachment in which material possessions have no relevance any more:

Attachments gone, deliverance won,
His thoughts are fixed on wisdom:
He works for sacrifice (alone).

And all the work he ever did
Entirely melts away

The Bhagavadgita

According to the Bhagavadgita, work should be done in a spirit of complete detachment; it is the detachment that counts, not the work. Detachment leads to 'liberation', and the self, once liberated, sees the essential irrelevance of work. It is detachment that would lead to happiness and contentment and the road to that state of mind is through work.

This is where we need to look at eastern philosophies and practices in greater depth, and yoga comes in as a practical guide to help us lead contented lives. With a little effort and training (to begin with you need a yoga master to guide you, especially with the breathing exercises, pranayama, which forms the core of all yoga practices), each one of us can observe every part of his or her body and feel the sensations that go through it. We soon learn that the sensations are linked to our minds: mental changes are reflected in changed sensations and sensations induce mental changes. By observing ourselves closely (an experienced yoga master will teach you how to stand 'outside' yourself), we can find the truth about the universe: that everything is transitory, built on waves that rise and fall very quickly. That is, there is no solidity; nothing that will be called: 'I, Me, Mine.' Our dissatisfaction and unhappiness come from denying this reality, from craving for, and clinging to, the things we want. When we understand the impermanent, transitory nature of things we want, we free ourselves from the causes of unhappiness; from focusing on ourselves we are able to move on and lead fully harmonious lives, good for ourselves as well as for those around us.

It is clear that a great deal of what we describe as happiness or being at peace in the cut and thrust of life comes from a sense of discipline – nothing in excess but always with a sense of balance.

Our happiness, as also our unhappiness, comes from our own volition and our own reactions – constantly liking this, disliking that; wanting this, not wanting that – without realizing that our reactions are impermanent, transitory phenomena. Put another way, we don't want economists to tell us how to assess our happiness or for governments to promote schemes that would enhance our sense of well-being. It is entirely our own self-reliance and our own understanding of, and coming to terms with, the world around us that will promote a sense of equanimity within us.

What follows from such an approach is that an objective measurement of happiness is not possible as it is a highly subjective sensation based on our totally subjective perception of reality, a perception is constantly changing due to multiple internal and external factors. It is not surprising that economists and politicians (most of whom have failed to 'deliver the goods' as they had promised) who claim to be the new 'gurus of happiness' have done so because they want to maintain the consumerist society they have created, which is based on tantalizing marketing gimmicks apart from profit and annual rates of growth. But happiness can't be quantified – if could be, it would only be a temporary measure that would demand more goods and services (to fulfil materialistic desires) with every passing moment.

***

The debate between the Western and Eastern approaches towards the concept of happiness and ways of achieving a state of equanimity is endless: while the former concentrates on the material conditions of life, the latter, while not entirely discarding the tangible world, emphasizes on the metaphysical factors that promote happiness. The Eastern approach believes that when midnight strikes and the coach turns into a pumpkin, people forget how happy they were, and that the wise ones have always warned us that the illusion would never work. But this doesn't square with their concept of happiness, which should be a condition where the mind is unpolluted like a lotus leaf, unaffected by the filth in the swamp around it.

Does all this amount to nothing more than going round in circles, trying to square the circle? Is there no simple answer that ordinary folk can understand? Many gurus and swamis and babas and matajis of the happiness industry have stressed on simplicity, or being true to your inner self, as the road to be followed, as summed up in the following lines:

> [Be to yourself] as true as truth's simplicity
> And simpler than the infancy of truth.

William Shakespeare: Troilus and Cressida

his holiness the 14th dalai lama
(tenzin gyatso)

THE ART OF HAPPINESS

Happiness is about attitude, calm mind, no stress, no anxiety, no fear. At one level you see negative things, but at a deeper level, you can have a combined perspective, irrespective of whether you are a religious believer or a non-believer.

EVERYONE WANTS A HAPPY LIFE. I DO NOT THINK anybody wakes up in the morning and wishes for trouble. Yet there are many problems that are of our own creation. Why? Not knowing the reality due to lack of a holistic view, and from the Buddhist viewpoint, grasping at things. Another reason is a self-centered attitude. We must realize the actual reasons for our problems without blaming them on external causes. Now, how do we remove them? Not through prayer, money, or power, but through understanding, awareness, wisdom.

Happiness is as much a part of our mind as sadness. Usually, people have the impression that the mind is something independent and absolute. I have met many scientists, but the distinction between sensorial mind and mental consciousness is still not clear. People seek pleasure mainly at the sensorial level. For example, beautiful things seen by the eye consciousness, beautiful music heard by the ear consciousness, and also taste, smell, and sex. These examples of positive experiences mainly for the senses are temporary.

At the mental level, if we develop a positive experience, it is long-lasting and it is possible to create a calm, peaceful, pleasant feeling. Physical illness or pain too can be subdued with mental calmness. However, if at the mental level there is fear, anxiety or stress, these cannot be subdued by pleasant experiences at the sensorial level. By paying attention, everybody can experience this. I think happiness mainly lies in a sense of satisfaction. Physical suffering and painful experiences might bring deep satisfaction at the mental level. Happiness mainly refers to the consciousness level, the mental level.

All major religions try to bring calm, peace and positive feelings at the mental level. Religions have one practice in common – faith – not at the sensorial level but at the level of consciousness, though it might help to listen to devotional music or look at an image. Love and compassion, with forgiveness, tolerance and contentment, also are at the level of consciousness.

Jainism and Buddhism are non-theistic religions that believe in the law of causality – cause and effect – and not in a creator. Karma means 'action'. Any action – physical, verbal, mental, out of some emotion or motivation – is karma. There is positive karma when the motivation is good, based on concern for others' wellbeing, and is of benefit to others and oneself. There is no absolute positive or negative. Negative motivation means that ultimately it will bring something uncomfortable to oneself or to others. Experiences of pleasure and pain are due to karma. Though the approach of theistic and non-theistic religions might be different, their aim is the same – to strengthen love, compassion, forgiveness. If you do good to others, you will benefit. If you harm others, you will face negative consequences. Based on facts, we can see that warm-heartedness – affectionate heart or compassionate heart – is the source of happiness.

Biologically, among all social animals there is some sense of responsibility towards a group. Individuals' survival and happiness depends on this. Our wellbeing depends on that of the rest of the group. Because of this, there is concern for the group we belong to. The emotion that brings the group together is affection, love, compassion. By nature, we feel affection and compassion to protect our interests. Using our intelligence, we can increase this love and compassion beyond the biological level, where it often goes with hatred or suspicion.

The second level of compassion, developed through training, uses reason, logic, and a wider perspective, to become unbiased. For example, the biological level of compassion can develop towards your friend but not towards your enemy because it is oriented towards the other's attitude. Your friend's attitude towards you is good, so you feel love. Your enemy's attitude to you is harmful, therefore you feel anger. We can use our intelligence to think that irrespective of whether the individual is a friend, enemy, or neutral, he or she is still part of the community. We must consider the rest of humanity, the rest of the world, as part of us because our interest depends on them. We can feel genuine concern for others' wellbeing because they are part of our community, irrespective of their individual attitudes towards us. We, human beings, using our intelligence, have the potential to develop that level of compassion.

In terms of genuine compassion, it is important to make a distinction between the other's action or attitude, and being itself. If your enemy creates problems for you, as far as the action is concerned, you might condemn it, but only as an action. You can still have compassion and concern for the other's wellbeing. In fact, if you let their wrongdoing continue without check, they too will suffer. Condemnation out of concern, in order to stop their wrongdoing, is actually compassion at work. Training, by utilizing our intelligence, and analyzing, can enable us to change. Once we develop a mental attitude that is more realistic, open, based on reason, then we can feel happiness. Happiness is about attitude, calm mind, no stress, no anxiety, no fear. At one level you see negative things, but at a deeper level, you can have a combined perspective, irrespective of whether you are a religious believer or a non-believer.

Scientific findings often link a healthy body with a healthy mind. No matter what the circumstances, if you can keep a calm mind, it benefits your health. Scientists tell me that fear, anger, hatred eat away at our immune system, while keeping our minds calm is helpful to strengthening our immune system. Once in New York, at a meeting with scientists, one of them mentioned that people who often use 'I, me, my likes' have a greater risk of heart attack. Their self-centered attitude makes even small problems appear unbearable.

Once you develop an open heart, and a concern for others' wellbeing, an inner door opens. Then you can communicate with others easily. It brings more friends, reduces loneliness, and a more compassionate attitude is useful for our health. This mental attitude is attuned with our realities as a social animal.

Talking of my own experience, now I am 77. At 16, I lost my freedom. At 24, I became a stateless, homeless refugee. I lost a small house – Tibet, but found a big house – India. My life has been turbulent, but comparatively, my mind is peaceful. During the turbulences of my life, my mind has remained comparatively calm. The immediate result is that my health is good. If a human being uses intelligence properly, the result mentally is happiness and physically is health. Everybody has this potential.

* * *

I am often asked as to what is the difference between love and compassion. I do not know the exact difference between them. In Sanskrit, there is the word *karuna;* and in Tibetan, there are two words, *inji* and *chamba.*

Chamba means a desire to have happiness, whereas *karuna* and *inji* mean the desire to overcome suffering.

Genuine compassion does not depend upon whether the other is nice to me; it is based on the realization and acceptance that the other is also a central being and has the right to be happy and overcome suffering, irrespective of his or her attitude to me. Even an enemy who is harming me is a central being and has every right to overcome suffering, to achieve happiness. So, genuine compassion is a sense of concern for everyone. Compassion is not pity; it is based on respect for the other's rights and a recognition that the other is just like myself.

You may well ask that if compassion is, then, virtuous and desirable, how does it make me a happier or a better human being?

I will answer this with an example. When I meet someone on the street, I am reassured of my human feelings. Regardless of whether I know him or not, I smile at him. Sometimes there is no response; sometimes there is suspicion. But I get the benefit of smiling. Whether the other person gets any benefit or not depends upon his own thinking as well as on the circumstances.

The rewards of practicing compassion go first to the practitioner. I believe it is very important to understand this; otherwise, we will believe that compassion benefits the other and has nothing for us. A compassionate attitude helps you communicate easily with fellow human beings and other central beings. As a result, you make more genuine friends; the atmosphere is more positive, which gives you inner strength. This inner strength helps you voluntarily concern yourself with others, instead of just thinking about your own self.

Somebody once asked me: 'You have carried the burden of the suffering of your people and your homeland for so many years. Yet you carry a lightness of being, a spontaneous joy, that touches all whom you meet. How do you do this?' My answer was simple: 'Nothing special! Good sleep, good food! I don't think it is one particular thing, but it is the attitude toward oneself, toward others. Life is not easy from the Buddhist point of view. This body is a hindrance; negative karma or samsaric karma can create problems. You also sometimes see unfortunate things happen. But unfortunate things can be transformed into a positive event; you can use them to gain experience. Therefore, they are helpful in daily life. Of course, one must avoid negative consequences from the beginning. But once something happens, try to look at it from different perspectives. For example, we have lost our country. This situation, however, also presents new opportunities; if you look at it from a positive aspect, the frustrations become less.

What is this change of attitude that makes a person feel happy? As a Buddhist monk, my main aim is to practice altruism, the practice of bodhicitta, with wisdom or awareness. I believe that analytical meditation is one of the key methods to transform the mind and the emotions. This has brought me inner peace and strength. Such a method also allows one to change perceptions and attitudes toward oneself, others, and immediate problems. I feel that the foremost change would be that as one develops a sense of concern, of compassion for others, one's mind broadens or widens. At that point, an individual's problems and suffering appear very small.

How do we develop concern for others and for ourselves? One could start by analyzing the value of negative feelings, or ill feelings, toward others. Consider what that means to you, and how you feel about yourself. Next, probe the value of such a mental attitude and the value of a mind that shows concern and compassion for others. I am suggesting you analyze and make comparisons between these two mental attitudes. From my experience, I have found that insecurity and a lack of self-confidence brings about fears, frustrations, and depression. However, if your nature changes to a selfless concern for the welfare of others, you will experience calmness, a sense of inner strength, and self-confidence. The capacity for compassion that one has for others is the measuring rod for one's own mental state, and compassion develops an inner strength. It is unnecessary to see the results of our acts of compassion. In some cases, our sense of compassion may not be appreciated.

Many people have the impression that the practice of love, compassion, and forgiveness is of benefit to others, but will serve no specific purpose to one's own self. I think that is wrong. These positive emotions will immediately help one's own mental state.

The Buddhists have a fascinating attitude toward what

is called the 'enemy.' For instance, some monks pray on mats that have the message PRAY FOR THE CHINESE on them. For genuine Buddhist practitioners, the enemy of the community presents a real opportunity to practice patience and tolerance. In order to improve genuine compassion, the practice of tolerance is essential. For the practice, the enemy is very important. That's one way to look at it.

In the Mahayana school of Buddhism, we refer to other beings as mother-centered beings. There is no point in excluding those people who create trouble. In our case, our Chinese brothers and sisters are also mother-centered beings; hence, we have to consider them. There is one good example of a monk who spent more than 17 years in a Chinese prison, or labour camp. He had been with me before 1959. In the late 1980s, he joined me in Dharamsala. Because we know each other very well, I asked him about his experiences. He said that on a few occasions he faced real danger. I assumed that he meant danger to his life. 'What danger?' I asked.

'The danger of losing compassion for the Chinese' was his answer. I think this is a very wonderful thing to say. I think that is the reflection of the practice. Not all Tibetans share this view. One day I asked a Tibetan from my own village whether he felt angry with the Chinese. Before his answer or words came, his cheeks began to shake and his face became red. He said: 'Of course, yes.' So, such people are also there. There are all kinds of people.

* * *

I recite the Eight Verses of Thought Transformation every day. I had received an oral transmission and teachings on the verses from Trijang Rinpoche. Although I cannot spend much time on them, I usually recite and think a little about them. This is something very useful. The composer of this text is Kadampa Master Geshe Langri Thangpa. The great master of Dharma saw the practice of bodhicitta, exchanging self with others, as the most important part of his practice. I shall explain these verses briefly.

1. With the determination to accomplish the highest welfare of all sentient beings, who excel even the wish-granting jewel, may I at all times hold them dear. The kindness of sentient beings toward us is not merely confined to the achievement of our final goal: enlightenment. The fulfillment of our temporary aims, such as the experience of happiness and so on, also depends on their kindness. Therefore, sentient beings are superior even to the wish-fulfilling jewel. We say the prayer *May I be able to hold them dearer than the wishfulfilling jewel.*

2. Whenever I associate with others, may I think myself the lowest of all and from the depth of my heart hold the others supreme. When we meet others, we should not think of ourselves as superior and look down on them or pity them, but see them as the source of our happiness. We should hold them dear and revere

them because they have the equal capacity of the activities of the Buddha, like granting us happiness and enlightenment.

3. In all actions, may I search my mind, and as soon as delusions arise, endangering myself and others, may I firmly face and avert them. When we engage in such noble practices, we might encounter obstacles. These are not external but internal. They come from our own minds; they are delusions of our own minds. The real enemy is within us, not outside. When we are able to discipline and control the mind through training and effort, we will gain real peace and tranquility. When the mind is out of control, we lose our inner peace, our happiness, immediately.

    Ultimately, the constructive power is within us, as is the destructive power. So it rests in our own hands. The Buddha said, therefore, you are your own master, and everything depends on your mind-set.

    In the practice of bodhicitta, we have to refrain from all types of nonvirtues. Primarily, we must avoid anger. Anger can never produce happiness, whereas attachment can bring about the experience of happiness, in certain cases. Therefore, for someone who practices bodhicitta, the biggest enemy is anger. We have a saying in Tibet: *if you lose your temper and get angry, bite your knuckles.* This means that if you lose your temper, do not show it to others. Rather, bite your *own* knuckles.

4. When I see beings of wicked nature, pressed by violent nonvirtues and afflictions, may I hold them dear as if I had found a rare and precious treasure. When many people are excited by emotional afflictions and pressed by delusions, Sravaka and Pratyekabuddhas – practitioners of the Hinayana vehicle – tend to avoid them because they are afraid of getting involved and carried away themselves. Bodhisattvas, on the other hand, face them bravely and take their chance in bringing happiness to other sentient beings.

5. When others out of envy treat me badly with slander, abuse, and the like, may I suffer the defeat and offer the victory to them. When other beings, especially some who hold a grudge against you, abuse and harm you out of envy, you should not abandon them, but hold them as objects of the greatest compassion and take care of them. The practitioner should absorb the loss himself or herself and offer victory to the others. Practitioners of bodhicitta do this not with the intention of becoming virtuous, but rather with the motivation of helping other sentient beings.

6. When the one whom I have benefited with great hope hurts me badly, may I behold him as my supreme guru. When from among those who have a personal grudge against you, there is someone whom you have helped and he repays your kindness in a wrong way, you might feel that you do not want to help him

ever again. It is very difficult not to hold this against him, and this becomes a great stumbling block for the practitioner of altruism. However, a practitioner should care specially for such a person. A person who harms you must also be seen as someone who is your spiritual guide. You will find that your enemy is your supreme teacher.

7. In short, may I directly and indirectly offer the benefit and happiness to all my mothers. May I secretly take upon myself the harmful actions and sufferings of my mothers. Everyone wishes to achieve happiness and to avoid suffering. When we remember that others are infinite in number and you yourself are only one, no matter how superior you are, others become more valuable. And if you have some power of judgement, you will find that it is worthwhile to sacrifice yourself for the sake of others. One person must not sacrifice an infinite number of others for the sake of himself.

    At this point I usually recommend a special visualization. See yourself as a very selfish person, and in front of you a great number of sentient beings are undergoing suffering. To get an even clearer picture of sentient beings, visualize them actively experiencing their sufferings. You yourself remain as a third person, neutral and unbiased. Then see which side you want to take. Analyze which one is more worthwhile – the welfare of one person or the welfare of many beings. If they thought like this, even the most selfish politicians would, without hesitation, join the majority. How sad it is to be selfish!

One who practices taking onto himself all the sufferings and faults of all other sentient beings from the depth of his heart also trains in sharing with others all the good qualities such as virtues and happiness that he has in himself. Train yourself. Initially it is very difficult for your selfish attitude to decrease, and you cannot control it easily. But if you persevere for a long time, you will be successful.

The first seven verses deal with the practice and method of Conventional Bodhicitta, and the eighth verse deals with the practice of Ultimate Bodhicitta wisdom.

8. May all this remain undefiled by the stains of the eight worldly principles; may I, by perceiving all dharmas as illusory, unattached be delivered from the bondage of cyclic existence.

If someone undertakes such a practice motivated by worldly concerns such as wishing for a long and healthy life, happiness, and perfection in this life, it is basically wrong. And if someone practices hoping that people might call him a great religious practitioner and so forth, it is definitely wrong. And if someone practices bodhicitta, altruism, and views all the objects of his compassion or all sentient beings as truly existent, that is also wrong.

You should undertake this practice with the understanding that all phenomena are illusions. One understands that all phenomena are illusions by the force of having refuted or negated their true existence. What is left behind is mere imputation—mere label and designation, which are illusions. Although they appear as though truly existent, they lack true existence.

* * *

Happiness, nirvana, or moksha is freedom from suffering, from negative emotion, from the serfdom of ignorance. This is the concept of Dharma, especially in Indian philosophy, where liberation from ignorance – happiness – is the goal. All beings are equal in the sense that all, including animals, have a right to be happy.

People believe that economic difficulties, illiteracy, and ill-health lead to unhappiness. They pay a lot of attention to material development. However, even in the developed countries of the West, people are experiencing loneliness, anxiety, and fear deep inside, often due to greed, discontent, and mental unrest. Neither money nor technology can help to develop inner peace, which requires the right kind of mental attitude. The problems are caused by human intelligence, and we must find the answer also within human intelligence.

Today, scientists inform us that increased movements in certain parts of the brain are positive. Soon people will realize that inner tranquility is based on a more open mind and heart, a sense of concern toward all humanity as one entity. With such a concept, to achieve our own happiness we have to respect the rights of others to be happy. This may seem idealistic, but human history has shown us that many things that have looked unrealistic as a blueprint have worked out eventually.

We want happiness, the happiness that comes from within us – inexpensive, isn't it? A happiness and peace that nobody can destroy, steal, or take away. This inner peace is most precious. The basis of inner peace is love and compassion. If you agree, implement it; if you do not agree, that is all right, too.

deepak chopra

THE HAPPINESS TRAP, AND
HOW TO AVOID IT

When you don't need money, status, power, or even other people to love you, those things don't vanish. They remain valuable as mirrors of your inner fulfillment. Or to put it simply, the externals that people chase after are the byproducts of happiness, not the cause.

I'VE BEEN THINKING A LOT RECENTLY ABOUT HAPPINESS. It's a subject not many people devote themselves to. Until the advent of 'positive psychology' in the last decade, the psyche was largely studied through the window of unhappiness. Psychologists had their hands full treating anxiety, depression, obsessive-compulsion disorder, and a host of other maladies the mind is heir to. It was assumed that happiness didn't need much thought, on the whole. When pollsters asked the simple question: 'Are you happy?' more than 80 per cent of Americans say yes.

But there's a hidden trap behind this cheerful response. The expansion of happiness is the goal of life. However you define success, if it didn't bring a measure of happiness, success wouldn't be worth attaining.

So what kind of success would make a person truly, deeply, and permanently happy? Society pressurises us to believe that external achievement is the key. If you attain enough money, status, power, and all the other trappings of a burgeoning career, you will experience happiness. To this list most people would also add the need for fulfilling relationships and a secure family life.

The trap is that external success doesn't lead to happiness. The evidence is well documented by now. Winners of the lottery turn out to be largely miserable a few years after their windfall, with the vast majority saying that they wish they had never won. Studies of wealth reveal that beyond a certain modest prosperity, having more money not only doesn't buy greater happiness, it tends to make people unhappy. On the broad scale the traffic in pharmaceuticals for depression and anxiety is a multibillion-dollar business (Prozac opened the floodgates of psychotropic drugs that individually break the billion-dollar mark). Divorce rates hover around 50 per cent, meaning that anyone's chances of attaining a happy marriage are no more than random.

Standing back from this confusing picture, I began to think of one person who had the courage to test, through his own experience, almost every avenue that might lead to happiness. He came to a definite conclusion, and he did it 2,500 years ago. First he tried the avenue of wealth and privilege. Born a prince, he was carefully protected from any form of external suffering, yet by the time he grew up, simply the sight of other people's suffering convinced him that money and privilege were fragile and unreliable. Every person, he reasoned, must confront disease, aging, and death. Those threats were enough to undercut the comforts of the most coddled lifestyle.

Therefore, he turned to a simpler existence. He left his family and wandered the countryside, begging for alms and depending on the kindness of strangers. He had no worldly obligations anymore, and since he was still young and strong, the wandering life wasn't a hardship. He enjoyed the simplicity he had found, but his mind refused to be tamed. It ran riot with subtle fears and anxieties. He regretted many things in his past and worried about what the future might hold.

So he decided to tame his mind once and for all, which also involved taming his body, because the body carries out the mind's rampant desires. Through rigorous discipline, he underwent one kind of purification after another. He carried this out until his body wasted away and he was on the brink of death. Yet even when he was little more than a skeleton, his mind refused to be tamed. He crawled back to a normal existence, and as he recuperated from his ordeals, he wondered what path was left to him.

By now, you may realize that we are talking about Siddhartha Gautama, the ancient Indian prince who became the Buddha. As a physician myself, I think of him as a kind of soul doctor, someone who was willing to test to the fullest what it means to be alive and conscious. Siddhartha wasn't a conventional success story. He spent year after year in dissatisfaction, searching for one thing: a happiness that cannot be taken away. And year after year that kind of happiness eluded him.

Untill he attained enlightenment. The awakening of the Buddha is said to have taken place sitting under a tree on a moonlit night. Other than that, the whole thing seems exotic and strange. How can total transformation take place instantly after years of searching? Having found the goal of life -- supreme happiness that can never be taken away -- the Buddha must be called an ultimate success. I'd like to suggest that the exotic aura surrounding him is misleading. What turned Siddhartha into the Buddha is actually quite simple: he discovered his true self.

I am not a Buddhist; rather, his story is symbolic of everyone. Happiness is a universal goal, and if the Buddha's soul experiment was valid, the true self that he found is always available. By true self I mean a level of awareness that is happy without reasons to be happy. It enjoys a permanent state of fulfillment, needing no externals. When you don't need money, status, power, or even other people to love you, those things don't vanish. They remain valuable as mirrors of your inner fulfillment. Or to put it simply, the externals that people chase after are the byproducts of happiness, not the cause.

That's where my recent thoughts led me, to the notion that enlightenment is actually the simplest and most basic way to be happy. The term enlightenment sounds daunting and perhaps alien. It conjures up images of monks who have abandoned the world to worship God. But Siddhartha had already exhausted that avenue. He found that pursuing his true self, as directly as possible, was the route to happiness.

What does that involve? First, knowing what your goal is and not wavering from it. Second, meditating so that you can go inward to meet yourself. Third, daily patience and forgiveness. The mind does lots of strange things before it finds what it is looking for. Finally, a sense of union with everyone else who is seeking happiness, because true communion lies in realizing how similar all paths really are. As I see it, enlightenment is not only a normal state, it's the most normal state of existence. It's also the highest definition of success.

his holiness the 17th karmapa (trinley
thaye dorje)

———◦◦⋅⋅◦⋅◦⋅⋅◦◦———

HAPPINESS IS SIMPLE

Just talking about happiness is not going to make it happen. The first step is to work on ourselves, not to try to change others.

Y ES, HAPPINESS IS SIMPLE.
We don't have to order happiness from outside. We just have to look at our own goodness and our own qualities. Contentedness is the best of wealth. Happiness means having goodness and virtue within our own mind.

Just the air we breathe to keep alive is amazing; and you just breathe in and think this is happiness. Just breathing and remembering, is itself happiness. If we remember that, we appreciate what we have. Having a good human life is simple. Samsara has a lot of problems. If we can be expansive and open, that is what is going to bring us happiness in this life. If we cling to external things it will be difficult to have happiness. It's more a question of what we are or are not than what we have or don't have.

The outside conditions do not make a critical difference. It's not money. A beggar has time to sing but a rich man has to count his money. It is not fame and fortune. Celebrities don't have as much fun as the fans clapping and cheering for them. It's not sensations of pleasure.

Happiness comes when we familiarize ourselves with our own good qualities. Suffering is not the unpleasant things we see or hear. It is the afflictions that disturb our mind, the non-virtues. We need to have happiness in our lives. We need to take the seeds of the virtue and increase them. We need to decrease the afflictions.

We have closed the door on the nature of how things are. Go out, extend yourself to others, interact with others. We have shut out the opportunity to think about it. This comes out of our ignorance, clinging to ourselves. We need to take a metal hammer and smash it to bits. We need to have interest in and respect for all things. This is what the aim of dharma practice is. We need to develop a more profound understanding of how things are. We only think about things in a very limited way. We need to think in a vast way. We need to know it from within ourselves. That is how we need to practice emptiness. That is the aim of all our dharma practice.

Just talking about happiness is not going to make it happen. The first step is to work on ourselves, not to try to change others. One good person in the world is a big contribution. When we have developed ourselves only then will it benefit others. Doing it prematurely will bear no result whatsoever. While I cannot fulfil others in accordance with the wishes of the Buddhas and do little with my body and speech, yet with my mind I can generate feelings of affection and care. If you have had the real practice of mind training, you can transform obstacles into the path of enlightenment. This is a way to purify and remove our misdeeds.

Since I was a young child, I was pushed forth by the force of karma. When they came to me and said you're the Karmapa, I said ok. When they asked me to teach I said ok. My whole life has proceeded from the force of karma, not from my own intentions.

I was born in this world and live in this world with all its joys and pleasures. I have a lot of affection for this world, especially with the humans. I wish them all to be happy. I have affection to all you sentient beings who have been around for so many thousands of years. I would like to offer you this affection. There are so many natural disasters, we don't know what will happen in the future. We need to be satisfied with what we have and not think too much about the future. It is my hope that you may all be happy in this way.

Read the inscription to the caves at Ajanta which says a great deal: 'The joy of giving filled him so much it left no space for the feeling of pain.' *I hope through this message your happiness grows stronger and flourishes.*

his eminence the 12th chamgon kenting
tai situpa

———❖❖❖❖———

Achieving Happiness in
Challenging Times

Nobody achieves happiness forever, therefore nobody stops looking for it. We are born looking for happiness, and we die looking for it. So this is what samsara is.

The month of May is a very special month. In our tradition, it is the month in which the Buddha was born, attained enlightenment and also passed on into *Paranirvana*. In one month, all three very holy occasions took place. Hence, I'm very happy to write for the readers of this volume about this sacred dharma in this auspicious month, by a coincidence, on the sixth day of the month which will have a full moon – the 'full *nyingma*' – a time of celebration in India and all over the world. So first of all, my auspicious greetings to all the readers.

'Achieving happiness' is a very interesting phenomenon because when you achieve happiness, you 'become the happiness'. The times, challenging or not, no longer matter. People all over the world try to achieve happiness, and that is why they work day and night. Deep inside, all of us have the same meaning and purpose of achieving happiness. But when we try to define what happiness really is, each person's definition is slightly different. Also, a person's definition of happiness in different stages of life is also slightly different. Not only that, for some of us, what our definition of happiness was yesterday is at times different from what it is today or will be tomorrow, so that way happiness is a dualistic perception and it is what we all try to achieve.

Nobody achieves happiness forever, therefore nobody stops looking for it. We are born looking for happiness, and we die looking for it. So this is what samsara is. Samara means going in circles; we go in circle for achieving happiness. Even though everyone's definition of happiness might be slightly different, they all want to achieve happiness, then that principle for everybody is the same because our ultimate potential – our ultimate essence – does not have any limitation and therefore any kind of limitation is considered as suffering. For example, a poor person who doesn't have food or shelter is suffering from the limitation of having nothing to eat and no place to stay. So that person tries to find shelter and food to overcome that limitation. Once he has achieved that, he will be happy, but that happiness will not last forever because there are all kinds of shelters and food available, and he would struggle for better ones than what he has already got.

I'm using the example of food and shelter because these are very basic but there're many other things that we want beside these two. So that way, achieving happiness goes on. This scenario is, of course, quite poor because this somehow prevents us from contentment. This somehow always makes us suffer and struggle, but the reason why we are like that is because our potential has no limitation. So long as there is a limitation, we would want to overcome it. When you think about a simple thing like money, $1,000 is a very, very big amount for those who have nothing. But others who already have $1,000, then $10,000 is something to look for. It goes on and on and on. Same is the case with power. First of all, you would like to be respected by people who you know and care for. Once you achieve that, you would want to be respected by more people who not only listen to you but also obey you. Something which is limitless cannot be, in any way, limited. So until we give up, the process of achieving happiness has no end. What makes us very happy today is already boring the following day.

When we talk about the 'challenging times', it becomes very clear that happiness is an illusion because we are unable to achieve something we truly want to, and have to struggle to get it. Also, just like us, others too would like to achieve the same or similar things, as a result of which it may be very difficult to do the same because of the many obstacles that one might have to face, like conflict in interests or other such reasons. All such scenarios and many others, including natural calamities, i.e., both disharmony among people and disharmony among nature, amount to challenging times.

If we look at samsara, with a sense of perspective, then it is always challenging. We don't have wings to fly, you know, and we have to do so many things to achieve one simple thing. For example, in the old days, people had to grow their own rice, dig the earth to get water, and plant seeds and then take care of the weeds, day after day. The challenges they had to face were floods, drought, wild animals, etc. Nowadays, however, majority of us don't have to grow rice. We just go to the grocery shop and buy it, and there are so many varieties to choose from. But now the challenge we face is that we have to pay much more than what we used to. While the income does not necessarily multiply, the cost of living certainly does. Then it becomes a challenge. Same happens when the number of persons living in a family increase, but number of persons generating income doesn't.

To put things together, achieving happiness is relatively impossible whether the times are challenging or not, because what a person wants can itself change in colour, shape, size and definition, each day. There is always something that we have to have, which we don't. Therefore, we can never achieve happiness, but what we can do is 'become that happiness'. Now when we find out that our potential has no limitation, from that moment, we try and find the answer to why we all want something to make us happy all the time. To find out what makes us happy or not so happy becomes less challenging, and we become less contented with things that make us happy, and less frustrated with things that don't. So we are not desperately trying to achieve happiness because we know we are limitless in our potential, and also at the same time there is no such thing as achieving the ultimate relatively; we can only achieve the relative relatively. If we try to achieve the ultimate relatively, we then will have to face all these challenges, all these pains and problems, and struggles and disharmony. So that is one way to look at this. Another way is to look at it as a challenge. As long as there is 'I' and 'me', there is a challenge. Now because there are over five thousand million others on this earth, there's always a challenge. If you realize that just like 'me', everybody else too wants to achieve happiness, then the desperateness and the personal agony for not achieving happiness the way 'I' want it becomes much less. And we can almost say that we will never be neurotic about achieving happiness the 'my way', because if all five thousand million human beings want everything 'my way', then one person's 'my way' may conflict with another's. So when one knows that, for the sake of oneself and, of course if you are more mature, for the sake of everyone else, one will stop acting so much centred around 'my way' because it is not good for you or others around you since 'my way' is on 'everybody's way'.

There are intellectual as well as some broader ways to look at the concept of achieving happiness in the challenging times as well – as a person who meditates and prays: a Buddhist or a person who already has something like Buddhism in his or her life. That is, everyday we say, 'May all sentient beings be free from suffering; may all sentient beings be happy.' These are the two of the four limitless thoughts. For example, when we say this everyday and mean it, the challenge becomes very weak, i.e., achieving happiness for oneself does not become a big deal. If seeing somebody else happy makes you happy, it is much better than being happy only when you are happy. But if you are that kind of a person who is only happy when you are happy, then there is likelihood that when anybody else is happy then that person will be unhappy. With less jealousy and envy, others' happiness becomes the cause and condition for one's own happiness.

Moreover, the 'challenging times' also become more positive because when people are suffering and when you have developed compassion, you see others' suffering and temporarily forget your own and, at times, help others overcome it or, at least, pray for them to overcome their suffering. Here, the challenge leads to ways and means for exercising your ability to alleviate others from pain and problems. I think you can also learn this from certain calamities, when people forget themselves and do everything to save others. So instead asking themselves, 'Why is this happening to me?' they just look around to find somebody in need and help out as long as they can. So with a good heart and, let's say, the dedication to do something good for others, the challenge and the suffering is not there anymore for you. I'm not saying that one should look for natural calamities to practise this. Definitely not! Natural calamities or any kind of man-made calamities should not happen. But if they do, and one does one's best to help others out, it will naturally make them overcome their own unhappiness.

In a similar way, when we practise meditation, then more of a challenge is better for our progress. For example, for meditation, many of us go to small areas with no noise and live in remote places where nobody's there. Such places are very easy, very quiet and very serene. But most of us live in the city, next to the metro and the highway, with trains, big trucks and all kinds of cars passing by all day. There's so much vibration. I am not talking about the energy sort of vibration, but the real sort of vibration. When the ground and the house shake and other such things happen, practising meditation becomes difficult. But then if you are able to meditate in such a condition then you become a really good meditator. I don't mean that you should look for an apartment right next to the metro or the train, but if that is what happens to you then that is a challenge for your quiet meditation.

This, however, doesn't have to be. It is like learning how to swim in the ocean instead of the swimming pool. However, if you can swim in the ocean then swimming in a swimming pool would be very easy because oceans have currents, waves and salty waters which hurt your eyes like pepper does. So this way, challenges of any type, from the point of view of motivation and meditation, can be turned into positive conditions. There is a saying in the bodhisattva scriptures: The ripening of bad karma is the purification of bad karma because if there is a bad karma when something negative is happening, and if you manage not to be negative about it, then your negative karma is purified. Of course, if you become negative about it, then you are creating more negative karma. Having said that, I certainly do not mean that you should look for trouble, suffering or problems so that you can overcome your bad karma. You don't have to worry about it. If there is bad karma it will show up in all kind of ways. We can never, let's say, by mistake, miss the ripening of good or bad karma.

A student once asked me:

'We have been living in these challenging times for a long time now, and I'd like to know how long would these last. Secondly, instead of we just sitting and waiting for the challenging times to blow over, what should we do or what kind of position should we take in terms of our attitude or even actions to help, speed up the process, push the bad things away from us all, and one thing we can do to bring in or bring closer more peaceful and prosperous times?'

I feel that there can be several kinds of challenges resulting from both natural and man-made calamities. So, in the event of a man-made calamity, we can bring in a lot to change and, let's say, overcome. But if it is a natural calamity, then there isn't much we can do physically or orally, but mentally we can do everything. However, much depends on the situation and the kind of challenges we are facing. As to how long this challenging time will last, in the context of world economy, world environmental degradation, etc. then each and every one of us, if we do our best, can definitely make a difference. It is very easy for anyone of us to say: 'I'm just one of the five thousand million human beings; what I do will not make any difference.' If this is my attitude, then my friends' attitude will also be the same and in turn their friends' attitude too. Everybody on this earth is somebody's friend, so all of us should tell ourselves and our friends to take responsibility to make things better. For example, the economy and the environment are absolutely man-made, so although sometimes we blame untoward incidents on unfavourable weather conditions, droughts and other similar occurrences, all these are man-made and happen because of our lifestyle. If everybody is careful and mindful, the whole world will become so. And, eventually, all the conflicts, environmental problems, degradations, including economic degradations, ideology conflicts, etc., will vanish if everybody behaves themselves. And so we can do a lot.

As for the question, how long this will last, it will last as long as we let it happen and contribute to it, and will only change if we all do everything possible to change it, to turn it around.

I also recall someone asking me:

> 'During these difficult times, as Buddhists, we dedicate our prayers to all sentient beings and at the same time we always think of the suffering that all these sentient beings go through. In a certain way, I become unhappy thinking of their suffering since all I can do is pray for them, but can do nothing, you know, physically, practically or financially. Can you give us some advice as to how we can balance our mind because it seems like I've got so attached with the suffering of other sentient beings. As a result, I become very unhappy?'

I'm sure there are many ways, but what I can tell you clearly is that ultimately nobody is suffering, you know, since ultimately everybody is Buddha. But relatively, everybody is suffering including you, me, and everyone else. Ultimately, you are Buddha, I am Buddha, everybody is Buddha, so therefore, you don't have to look at the problems in this world – problems and sufferings of other people – we don't look at it as an ultimate suffering. They are relative sufferings, so you are seeing them with wisdom. You do not pray for them desperately, but are praying for them with wisdom and with understanding. Once you know and understand that everybody is only suffering relatively because they don't have the realization of the ultimate, you will be able to strike a balance. For example, when something like a very precious porcelain article you possess breaks, it is very sad because that porcelain meant a lot to you, but now it is broken. But you should know that the porcelain, whether or not it is broken, ultimately it is the same thing. So that way, relatively, you are a little bit upset but you will not go crazy about it, or fight with somebody, or become very negative about it. You can even have a big laugh at it, you know: 'My precious porcelain is now broken, ha! ha! ha! ha!'

khushwant singh

TIME-TESTED TIPS

A good massage needs powerful hands going all over one's body from the skull to the toes. And if the hands are those of a female, that is even better and livelier. I have a massage done at least once a day.

COMING ON TO 98 AND STILL EARNING MORE THAN I did in my younger days, people ask me how I manage to do it. They regard me as an expert on the art of happiness. I have drawn up a list of few essentials which according to me are a must if you want to live happily.

1. *Good Health*

First and foremost is *Good Health*. If you do not enjoy good health you can never be happy. Any ailment, however trivial, will deduct from your happiness.

Whatever your age, it is very important to lead a regular life. Impose strict discipline on your daily routine and don't give yourselves any excuses. Even at my age, I still get up at 4.30 every morning, have breakfast exactly at 6.30 A.M., work through till lunch which is at noon, a short siesta ad then work again till 7 P.M. when it is my drink time, and supper at 8 P.M. sharp. I am not suggesting you to be a slave of your watch like me, but maintain regular hours.

As you advance in age, cut down on the intake of food and drink. I start my mornings with guava juice. It is tastier and more healthier than orange or any other fruit juice. My breakfast is one scrambled egg on toast. My lunch is normally *patli kichri* with home made *dahi* or a vegetable. I skip afternoon tea.

In the evening, what at one time used to be three pegs of scotch has now been reduced to a peg of single malt whisky. It gives me a false appetite. Before I eat supper, I say to myself: 'Do not eat too much.' I have always believed that a meal should have just one kind of vegetable or meat followed by a pinch of *chooran*. Moreover, it is best to eat alone or just with your family, and in silence. Talking while eating does not do justice to the food and you swallow a lot of it. For me, at my age, no more Punjabi or Mughlai food. I find South Indian Idli, sambhar and grated coconut easier to digest and healthier.

2. *Never Allow Yourself to be Constipated*

The stomach is a storehouse of all kinds of ailments. Our sedentary life tends to make us constipated.

Keep your bowels clean however you can: by having a glass of water first thing every morning, by laxatives, enemas, glycerin suppositories, whatever. Bapu Gandhi fully understood the need to keep bowels clean. Besides, taking an enema every day, he gave it to his women admirers also.

3. *Stop Complaining*

For those of you who are in old age, I would say *Stop Cribbing* about anything and everything, and just learn to cope with it. Make terms with it. Soon you will realize that a lot of it was only in your mind. Remember, as we grow older, we are less able to exercise our limbs. We have to devise ways to keep them active. Right into my mid-eighties, I played tennis every morning, did rounds of Lodhi Gardens in winters and swam for an hour in the summers. I am unable to do this anymore. The best way of overcome this handicap is regular massages. I have tried different kinds and was disappointed with the oils drip and smearing of oil on the body. A good massage needs powerful hands going all over one's body from the skull to the toes. And if the hands are those of a female, even better and livelier. I have a massage done at least once a day.

4. *Build a Healthy Bank Balance*

It need not run into crores but should be enough to provide for creature comforts and something to provide for recreation, like eating out, going to the pictures, travelling or going on holidays to the hills or by the sea. And, for the possibility of falling ill. A good bank balance will certainly help develop a peace of mind.

Shortage of money can be very demoralizing. Living on credit or borrowing, particularly from members of your inner family and children, is demeaning. It lowers one in one's own eyes. Hence, try and live within your own means.

5. *A Home of Your Own*

Rented premises can never give you the snug feeling of a nest which is yours for keeps that a home provides. If it has a garden space, all the better. Plant your own trees and flowers, see them grow and blossom, cultivate a kinship with them.

Once there are trees and flowers, a variety of birds, squirrels, butterflies and insects will follow. Perhaps, a cat or two may also walk in. They will all adopt you and believe me, give you immense joy and happiness. Your world will be full.

6. *An Understanding Companion*

A spouse, a live-in partner or a friend is essential. If there are too many misunderstandings, they will rob you of your peace of mind. If there are problems it is better to be divorced than to bicker all the time. To live together for the sake of children or for financial issues is just not worth it. In fact, it will make you more unhappy. You will feel a prisoner in your own house. So get out and move on. Live and live well. Only then will you be happy.

7. *Erase any Envy*

Please erase all envy towards those who have done better than you in life; risen higher, made more money, or earned more fame. Always remember, envy can be very corroding. Avoid comparing yourself with others. Look at those who are below you and not those above you. A Punjabi verse sums up:

> *Rookhi Sookhi Khai Kay Thanda Paani Pee*
> *Na Veykh Paraayee Chonparian Na Tarssain Jee*
> (Eat dry bread and drink cold water
> Pay no heed or envy those who smear their
>   chapattis with ghee)

8. *Avoid Gossiping*

Never allow other people to descend on you for gup-shup. By the time you get rid of them, you will feel exhausted and poisoned by their gossip-mongering.

9. *Take up Hobbies*

Cultivate some hobbies which can bring you a sense of fulfillment , such as gardening, reading, writing, painting, playing or listening to music. Going to clubs or parties to get free drinks or to meet celebrities is a criminal waste of time.

10. *Introspection*

Every morning and evening, devote 15 minutes to introspection. In the morning, ten minutes should be spent on stilling the mind and then five in listing things you have to do that day. In the evening, five minutes to still the mind again, and ten minutes to go over what you had undertaken to do.

11. *Never Tell a Lie*

Always keep your national motto in mind: *Satyamev Jayate* – only truth triumphs. Besides, unlike fibs and lies you never have to remember the truth.

12. Give Generously

Remember, you can't take it with you. You give to your children, servants or charity. You will feel better. There is great joy and happiness in giving.

13. Lastly, Avoid Prayers

Do not conform to the tradition of spending time in prayers and long hours rubbing your nose in places of worship. Or at the feet of some Babaji and Mataji, Swami, Guru and the likes. That amounts to conceding defeat. Instead, utilize that time in a hobby, growing bonsai, helping children of your neighbourhood with their studies.

A practice which I have found very effective is to fix my gaze on the flame of a candle, empty my mind of everything, and in my mind repeat : *Aum Shanti, Aum Shanti....* It does work. I am at peace with the world.

What I enjoy is solitude. It's the biggest secret of longevity. I'm fortunate I can spend a lot of time by myself. It is very beneficial to be alone. The mind gets an enormous amount of rest, and a day's silence gives you more energy. If you keep your mind blank for a while – and this is the sole purpose of meditation –

you can enjoy solitude and you'll find it empowering. The fact that I'm alone, and sit in silence for most of the day is like meditation. Till recently, when I used to go to Kasauli, I could be alone for weeks at a stretch, exchanging just a few sentences with the cook and gardener who double as caretakers. There's no television set there, and newspapers and a couple of neighbours were my only contact with the outside world. But I never missed human company, and was happy there. Now I am not able to make my regular trips to Kasauli, so I remain at home in Delhi. At times I sit in total silence, at times introspecting and happy in solitude.

Even when my wife passed away – we were married for sixty-two years – I sat like this, alone, all night, going over the past. Then, when people kept dropping in, it became tedious. I found it difficult to cope and went off to Goa. Today, my friends and contemporaries have all gone – all. I feel like a solitary traveller left on the road while others have fallen by the roadside.

I never thought of marrying again – not even when I became a widower. Even though mine wasn't a particularly happy marriage, the thought of marrying someone else didn't cross my mind. I've never wanted to be close to anyone. I've never believed in seeking advice or solace from someone or looking for someone to confide in. I don't like the idea of being emotionally dependent on people. I've always managed on my own, even during the worst crises. I don't sit back feeling depressed. Work is the cure of all ills.

There was a brief phase, when there was an injunction on the publication of my autobiography, when I was upset and angry. And the other time I felt low was when my marriage was going through difficulties and my wife threatened to leave me. I went to the Bangla Sahib Gurdwara and spent hours there trying to gather strength to deal with the crisis. But these were exceptions. Generally, I have never been depressed ... not even when I was sacked as editor of *The Illustrated Weekly of India*. I didn't go into depression but started writing a novel and it was writing that helped me go on. I'm emotionally strong. Even as a child I was known to speak my mind and have rarely ever lied. I hardly ever get angry or hassled. I think one lives a happier, longer life if one is able to get rid of irritants. No matter how big the setback, if you are able to say this one-liner, it helps: 'It doesn't matter . . . I don't give a damn!'

I have had my share of setbacks – and financial insecurities – in my earlier days. What helped me carry on is work. When I was sacked in that discourteous way I drowned myself in work. I decided to complete *Delhi*, which I'd been working on for some years. And after my wife passed away I immersed myself in more writing. I wrote much more than before. I believe in what the Quran and Hadith stress on: Don't waste time. Every single moment should be used. One cannot sit and brood.

Earlier, whenever I was tense, I used to go and visit the cremation grounds. It has a cleansing effect. But now I can't go anywhere. It's work that keeps me going. My writing has been a constant factor. I'm engrossed wholly in writing, and will be till the very end. There's no retirement for me. In fact, in my third year as editor of *The Hindustan Times*, when my contract was due for renewal, K. K. Birla asked me about my retirement plans – whether I'd like to retire. I told him rather categorically, that I'd retire only at Nigambodh ghat!

Nanthaniel Cotton (1707–88) sums up what I feel:

> If solid happiness we prize,
> Within our breast this jewel lies,
> And they are fools who roam.
> The world has nothing to bestow;
> From our own selves our joys must flow,
> And that dear hut, our home.

I wish all the readers of this volume long healthy lives full of happiness .

robert holden

———•◦ ༻✦༺ ◦•———

HAPPY ALREADY!

Unhappiness is a symptom of forgetfulness, as much as joy is a symptom of remembering. When we're unhappy, balance gives way, perspective collapses, faith falters, communication often breaks down, doubt doubles, panic ensues, and a thousand different symptoms spill all around us. The disharmony we feel is ultimately a disharmony with our self.

Picture the following scene:

I AM AT MY FRIEND JANE'S HOUSE. IT IS MIDAFTERNOON, and we are having tea. Jane and I are engaged in a deep and meaningful conversation when her two boys run into the room. They're young, full of energy, lively, and noisy. Tom is four years old, and Ben is three. Ben follows Tom everywhere.

Jane and I continue to talk, but soon we can't hear each other speak because the boys are in a dispute.

'What's the problem?' Jane asks.

Tom throws Ben off him, takes a deep breath, and says:, 'It's *my* turn to play on *my* bike, but Ben won't leave me alone, and he's already ridden *my* bike once today.' A few more things are said, but no agreement is reached.

'Go outside and sort this out. Robert and I are talking,'says Jane. The boys are dismissed.

After a minute or two, the boys run into the room again . . . with the bike! Before Jane can chastise them for bringing it into the house, Tom says: 'We've worked it all out.'

'Good,' we both say.

Tom continues: 'Today the bike belongs to me all day, and tomorrow the bike belongs to Ben all day.' Both boys nod their heads with great enthusiasm.

'Are you both agreed?' asks Jane, sounding quite surprised.

'Yes,' they both say.

'Good, now go along and play,' says Jane.

The boys turn around to leave, and just before they do so, Ben pipes up at the top of his voice: 'I know – let's pretend it's tomorrow!'

Tom and Ben's story illustrates perfectly how children use possibility thinking to enjoy happiness *now!* I believe that, contrary to popular opinion, a baby's favorite toy is not a thing, it's a moment – a moment called *now*. Children are born only with an awareness of *now* – past and future are meaningless at first. In the beginning, *now* is the whole world to children, their entire playground. This fascination and reverence for *now is* entirely natural; it is neither learned nor fabricated.

Kids like Tom and Ben are completely unimpressed

by the idea of 'future happiness' – above all, they want happiness *now!* Those who are yet to be indoctrinated or conditioned fully by meaningless 'laws of time' don't know how to wait for happiness. Why wait for heaven when the possibility for heaven exists right here and now?

I believe that as a young child, you too were alive to the infinite possibilities of the present moment. Like other children, you were full of wonder, imagination, awe, and appreciation for the precious present. *You got so much from 'now' because you gave so much to 'now'* – and for the entire time you were engaged with the present, you were happy to leave the past and future exactly where they were. *Now* was your treasure island, and you believed wholeheartedly that happiness was here and now, waiting to be seen. The more you believed this, the more you would look; and the more you looked, the more happiness you found. Here is an important key to happiness.

Milking the 'Sacred Now'

The world has changed greatly in recent times in an effort to accommodate our desire for happiness *now*. Everything has sped up. We live life fast – faster than ever. Fast technology, fast travel, fast careers, fast relationships, and fast results are all the rage in our 'I want it *now*' world. Indeed, the world is fast becoming a vast convenience store where you can get everything in an instant – instant coffee, microwave foods, minute-meals, half-hour film developing, 24-hour banking, drive-thru funerals, quickie divorces, television shopping, home delivery of everything, and, of course, instant credit. We're sold on signs that read 'No lines,' 'No need to wait,' 'One stop,' 'Open all hours,' and 'Buy now – pay later.'

One way of looking at our 'I want it now' world is to see it as a highly egotistical and selfish pursuit of happiness that is fueled by impatience, violence, and greed, doomed from the very start to 'end in tears.' Indeed, many people are voicing their concerns at 'the way the world is going,' believing that traditional values and morals are fast being corroded and obliterated by the chase for happiness now.

Another way of seeing our 'I want it now' world is that this clamour for happiness *now* reflects an instinctive wisdom and a great spiritual truth, which states that . . .

> *Everything – absolutely everything –*
> *is available to you 'now'.*

There's a famous story from the Zen tradition that tells of an encounter between a young, eager student and a well-respected Zen master, noted especially for his perpetual grace and happiness:

> 'Master, I dream of everlasting happiness. What is the highest wisdom you can teach me?' asked the student.

The master smiled. He took his brush and wrote, as if for the first time: 'Attention.'

'Wonderful,' said the student, 'and what comes next after attention?'

The master smiled. He took his brush and wrote, as if for the first time: 'Attention. Attention.'

'Yes,' nodded the student, utterly perplexed. 'Anything more?'

The master smiled. He took his brush and wrote, as if for the first time: 'Attention. Attention. Attention.'

'Okay, so what does "attention" mean?' asked the student, unable to see.

The master spoke: 'Attention means attention.'

'Is that all?' asked the student, obviously dispirited.

'Attention is all,' said the master. 'Without attention, happiness is nowhere; *with* attention, happiness is now here. Attention is freedom from all. Attention offers all.'

Every authentic school of wisdom and spirituality teaches you that *now* is the most abundant moment of your life. The bibles of the world, be it the Old Testament or the New, the Koran or the Bhagavad Gita, the Dhammapada or the Tao Te Ching – indeed, any true spiritual text – all agree that *now* is an eternal treasure chest dripping with beautiful, everlasting gifts of peace, happiness, love, and joy freely available to all on a 24-hour 'Don't pay now – don't pay later' basis.

Now is sacred! This is what the Zen master is trying to tell the eager young student in the story above. Indeed, talk to any spiritual teacher or guru worth their mantra, so to speak, and this person will tell you that *now* is always sacred. But why and how is *now* always sacred, you may ask? What if you've just been stood up on a date or you've just opened a bill or you've just chipped a tooth or your football team has lost again – how sacred is that?!

One approach to milking the *sacred now is* to place your attention on what is happening around you right at this minute and aim to appreciate, respect, and value it as much as you believe possible. You can do this right now. Before you read on, look around you and appreciate fully for a moment what your senses pick up. When you do so, you'll experience first hand how pleasurable appreciation can be. Events sometimes seem to make this exercise hard, but willingness can overcome this.

In my workshops for The Happiness Project, I often show a slide that reads:

HAPPINESSISNOWHERE.

When I ask people to call out what they can see, I always get two distinct answers, one being *happiness is nowhere*, the other being *happiness is now here*. Often, then . . .

the difference between 'happiness is nowhere'
and 'happiness is now here' has something to do
with the event, and everything to do with how
you see the event. Your perception is key.

The real secret to milking the *sacred now is* to place your attention not out in the world about you, but within yourself – your inner, unconditioned *Self.* In truth, the *sacred now is* an inner potential. It is eternal and abundant; and its geography is spiritual, not physical. In other words, the *sacred now* represents a permanent potential within you to experience love, freedom, and joy regardless of time, place, or circumstance.

The gift of happiness is wrapped in your heart, not the world. Thus, your happiness will never be mailed to you! And it can never get lost in the mail! In truth, your happiness has already been delivered, sitting in your inner mailbox – your heart – waiting to be opened. This is what the *sacred now is* really all about. In essence, then, you *are the key to happiness.* More than what happens to you, it is your perceptions, your thoughts, your beliefs, and your overall response that are essential; your Self, your original Self, is the real key.

The real reason *now* is so naturally abundant is because when you allow yourself to be unrestrained by fear and uninhibited by worry, it is *you* who is so naturally, originally abundant. In truth, then . . .

Now has enough wisdom to last you forever,
because within you, right now, there is all
the wisdom you listen for in others.

Now has enough love to last you a lifetime,
because within you, right now, there is the
love you continually cry out for.

Now has enough peace to last you an eternity,
because within you, right now, peace of mind
is one thought away at most.

And now has enough joy to outlast the world,
because within you, right now, the joy you
chase is not in things – it is in you.

The problem with our 'I want it *now*' society isn't that we want happiness *now*, but that we've lost sight of how to experience it now. In particular, we say, 'I want it *now*,' but we doubt and don't really believe that 'it is here *now*.' We've lost faith in *now* and have placed all of our faith in some imagined future. Similarly, we've lost faith in our *Self* and have placed all our attention on the world outside. Now it is the world, it seems, that must 'make us happy' – *and herein lies the source of all our misery.*

As long as you believe that it's the world that must make you happy, you leave yourself open to great disappointment and much sadness. Why? Because as long as you refuse to see your inner potential for happiness *now,* you will not see it in the world. *How can a mirror change the way you look?* Think about that, for the world is only a mirror. You will only see in the world what you're prepared to see in yourself – nothing more and nothing less.

Know, therefore, that the journey to true happiness and to happiness *now is* not a journey of physical distance or time; it is one of personal 'self-recovery,' where we remember and reconnect consciously to an inner potential for joy – a paradise lost – waiting to be found. One moment we look within and we see *happiness nowhere;* the next moment we look within and this time we see *happiness now here.* This is a revelation. This is enlightenment. This is joy!

The faster we chase the world and the future, the quicker we appear to overlook the possibility that happiness is here already. Every morning as we wake up, the alarm clock sings *'now,'* and from that moment on we do not give *now* another thought as we desperately chase our future. But are you so sure that happiness isn't already here with you *now?* Have you really looked? I mean, *really* looked?

Milking the *sacred now is* excavation work. It's about rediscovering an inner potential for original joy – a potential that already exists but has been buried beneath a pile of fears, doubts, guilt, conditioning, and history. Think of this potential for original joy not as something to arrive at, but as something you bring with you wherever you go. Recultivating this potential is our task, and the task begins with the realization that . . .

joy waits on welcome, not on time.

Diving for Treasures of the Soul

Psychology school taught me a lot about our potential – in particular, our potential for unlimited amounts of misery, pain, weakness, and despair! We studied every affliction, every neurosis, and every mental disease available at the time. In a nutshell, my psychology training consisted of: *Year 1,* an introduction to basic suffering; *Year 2,* the study of advanced suffering; and *Year 3,* a qualification in inspired suffering.

The focus was entirely on our inner potential to mess life up. My curriculum was the A–Z of suffering, from anger to zoophilia – including stress, depression, anxiety, neurosis, psychosis, neurotic-psychosis and psychotic-neurosis, hysteria, schizophrenia, obsessive-compulsive disorders, phobias, inferiority complexes, kleptomania, suicide, insanity, and delusion. At no time did we consider our potential for joy, love, or peace of mind. In effect, I was studying for a Ph.D. in misery!

Studying suffering full-time had a big impact on my way of thinking. I once read that history has no evidence that there ever lived a happy psychologist. I can see why now. After a while, I was able to work out just how low I was going to feel on any given day by looking at my lecture timetable. For instance, when we studied depression for a week, I remember that the entire class eventually felt totally depressed by the end. The same was true for any and all of the complexes, afflictions, disorders, and fixations. Getting an unexpectedly low mark for my paranoia essay didn't help at all!

Do you remember when in kindergarten or elementary school you were given a lecture on the importance of bodily hygiene and the dangers of head lice? And do you remember how, after 20 minutes of listening to this woman who showed you great big blown-up slides of head lice with six-inch teeth, you became absolutely convinced you had a nest of these things in your hair? Well, that's what it was like in my psychology lectures. Doctors-intraining will tell you that their experience was also the same.

I learned a very important lesson about perception and focus during those years, which is . . .

be careful what you look for because you will find it.

I immersed myself thoroughly in the study of misery. I received distinctions for the most part in every study I undertook. As I increased my focus, I soon realized that there was not *one* type of depression, but 100. Furthermore, there was not *one* sort of schizophrenia, but 30, 40, or more. Whatever you focus on, expands. Each day I hoped we might dive for pearls, but instead we merely collected crabs!

After a full six years of study, I still hadn't been given a single lecture on our potential for joy, peace, unity, wholeness, and success. Psychology, originally defined as *the study of the soul,* had been reduced to a study of illness and neurotic behavior. Freud and Behaviorism, in particular, reduced human beings to no more than a pitiful bag of blood and bones housing a mind full of neurotic defenses and endless psychotic potential for aggression and psychosexual hang-ups. Never was there any mention of the soul, of spirit, of divinity, of God, of love.

My training in psychology, with its almost exclusive focus on pain, is a very common story. It also reflects a tendency in our society to focus on negatives. Doctors, for instance, study illness, not health. Business leaders analyze failure, not success. Economists study cost, not value. Philosophers mostly debate original sin, not original blessing. Christians talk endlessly about crucifixion, not resurrection. Mental-health organizations publish books on 'Understanding Depression,' 'Understanding Stress,' and 'Understanding Bereavement,' but not on 'Understanding Joy' and 'Understanding Love.' The media is full of journalists suffering from an addictive, antisocial, obsessive-compulsive need to communicate and make up bad news. Literature and art is full of depressed poets and painters – can you name three joyful poets?

What you focus on most often becomes familiar, and what is familiar feels real to you. In our society, we focus on pain before joy, tears before laughter, and fear before love, so we gradually grow blind to our inner, ever-present potential for happiness. I remember well how my lecturers frowned on happiness. What they taught me essentially was: 'If you find that you're experiencing happiness – don't worry – you're just in denial and the pain will soon return!'

Happiness appeared to have no value, other than that it offered a temporary respite between periods of pain and trauma. It was defined simplistically as the absence of pain. Other messages I received included: 'Happiness is superficial, pain is deep,' 'Laughter is a common symptom of manic depression,' 'Smiling a lot means you're suppressing a hidden pain,' 'Optimism is often unrealistic and delusional,' and 'Talking to God is the first sign of a nervous breakdown.'

Of greater concern to me, though, is the large body of thought within the psychology profession that suggests that happiness is in some way a dysfunctional behavior in light of all the suffering in the world. The idea is: 'If you have normal blood pressure living in our troubled world, you're not taking it seriously enough.' There have been several recent studies that have tried to suggest that happiness is only an avoidance of real issues, a selfish coping strategy, or a superficial form of escape. This thinking doesn't take into account that your happiness is an inspiration, a gift to others, and a way out of suffering.

When I asked my lecturers why we didn't study happiness, they usually challenged me to look at my resistance to embracing my pain more fully! The most common explanation given, however, for why happiness, love, peace, and God aren't studied by psychologists is that they cannot be measured as easily as fear and pain. In other words, they are inner potentials that don't show up on laboratory apparatus designed to measure externals.

Just because psychologists choose not to focus on joy, however, doesn't mean to say that joy doesn't exist. We can refuse to look at the sun, for example, but that won't make it go away. One problem, though, with not focusing directly on happiness is that what has emerged in place of the truth is a myth of happiness where happiness has become *a potential time forgot,* clouded in misperception, superstition, doubt, and cynicism.

The Oasis in the Desert

It was while studying communications that I met a man in my class who was to change my life forever. His name was Avanti Kumar. Avanti was an Asian gentleman, a mature student of about 24 years old, and the spitting image of the actor Danny DeVito – short build, stocky, no hair directly on top of his head but wild curly bushes of growth either side, big bronzed cheeks, a great smile, and a beautiful and radiant light in his eyes.

Avanti always sat at the back of the class, and in the early weeks he was always last in and first out. 'Who is he?' we all wondered. All we knew about him was that he was quiet and that he was always smiling. In fact, he was never *not* smiling. It was as if he had a private joke running in his head all the time.

I was deeply intrigued by Avanti from the very first moment I laid eyes on him. It was as if I somehow knew him already. There was a familiarity I felt but couldn't explain. I remember wanting to talk to him but feeling, unusually for me, too nervous to approach.

I'll never forget our first conversation. I asked him why he'd chosen this course to study. His answer was: 'To meet you, of course.' His smile really was infectious.

After that, I made sure we drank coffee together most days. I asked questions, and he gave me cryptic clues. I remember asking him one day: 'What are you?'

'A yogi,' he replied.

'A what?' I asked.

'A student of yoga,' he said.

'Oh! You mean like Jane Fonda!' Fortunately, we enjoyed each other's humor. Soon, another student, Phil, joined our coffee sessions. We became inseparable. We were one.

It was as if Avanti was fresh out of some Himalayan cave or esoteric monastery, where, I imagined, he'd been sitting for centuries in blissful meditation. He was my first direct experience of someone consciously connected to, and aware of, the inner potential for joy – anywhere, anytime. Over the next few months, he carefully and lovingly reacquainted Phil and me with this inner awareness as we talked about yoga, metaphysics, spiritual wisdom, and the more enlightened schools of psychology.

'So far all you've learned about is a psychology of the ego, or lower self,' Avanti explained, 'which is immersed in separation, fear, and suffering. If you'd like, I will teach you about another psychology, a psychology of wholeness and of the Higher Self, which teaches you how to allow your inner joy to shine on the world once more.'

It was with Avanti, then, that I first began to focus directly on happiness. It was Avanti who first taught me that happiness is not just the absence of pain, but that . . .

true happiness is an inner power –
natural, healing, abundant, and always available.

Like all great teachers, Avanti loved to tell stories. One day he introduced me to the story of two birds, first written in an ancient Hindu text called the *Mundaya Upanishad*. It reads:

Two birds
    inseparable companions
    perched on the same tree.

One eats fruit,
   the other looks on.

The first bird is our individual self,
   feeding on the pleasures and
   pains of this world;
The other is the universal Self,
   silently witnessing all.

'Think of the two birds as two thoughts flying about in the sky of your mind,' said Avanti. 'The first bird, *the individual self,* is your ego. It 'desires' happiness, and it tells you that you must search the world to find it. The second bird, *the universal Self, is* your spirit. It 'knows' happiness, and it tells you that you are happy already, that you were created happy, that all the happiness you have ever dreamed of rests in the centre of your real *Self* right now.

'Like an oasis in the desert, the *universal Self* is wholly joyous, wholly abundant, and wholly peaceful,' said Avanti. 'It is home to the *sacred now,* your inner potential for immediate peace and joy anywhere, anytime.'

With Avanti's guidance, I immersed myself in Eastern and Western literature in an effort to understand further the concept of the *individual self* and the *universal Self.* There are many names for these two selves, some of which I've listed in Table A.

Table A

learned self	original Self
false self	real Self
fearful self	loving Self
critical self	creative Self
lower self	higher Self
dissociated self	unified Self
ego	holy spirit
split self	whole Self
body/mind	spirit/soul
persona	atman
flesh	christos
nothing	'I am'
sin	source
hell	heaven
fallen self	divine Self

Today, many years later, I now think of the universal Self as your unconditioned Self – the Self that exists behind the mask of your personal history, your conditioning, your learned limitations, the roles you play, your persona, your defenses, your doubts, and your fears. This unconditioned Self is the original you, untouched by the world, completely safe and whole. It is who you really are, and not who you have been taught you are by parents, teachers, friends, lovers, anybody else, and most of all, yourself.

Your unconditioned Self is the presence of peace. Three words, in particular, describe the unconditioned Self, and they are: (1) *wholeness;* (2) *love;* and (3) *joy.* The oriental mystics called the unconditioned Self the 'uncarved block.' Other names for it include the Zen term 'the original face,' the Buddhist phrase 'the sacred happiness,' the North American name 'free spirit,' the Taoists' 'inner smile,' and the Christian mystics' 'inner Eden.'

E.G.O. – *Everything Good is Outside*

The following story helps to describe the plight of the ego, or conditioned self:

Each morning at 4 A.M., Brother Daniel would be the first to rise in the monastery. He got up early by choice, and he was proud to do so. While his teacher and all of his brothers slept peacefully, Brother Daniel busily exerted great effort in his prayer, study, and meditation practices. Enlightenment was his goal.

Every day, Brother Daniel would pray longer and louder for enlightenment. He worked hard at improving his physical posture for meditation, and, above all, he would labor to memorize all of the ancient spiritual texts at the monastery. Rarely, if ever, did Brother Daniel rest, eat, or sleep, for he wanted to get to enlightenment and he wanted to get there fast. Brother Daniel liked to meditate and pray, but most of all, he immersed himself in scriptures. He liked to be quiet and still, but he rarely had time, for he found that there was always so much to do. He liked the silence, but he would rather hear his teacher talk of the silence.

Brother Daniel's teacher, a gentle, peaceful man who was always smiling, would encourage Brother Daniel to slow down, enjoy the sun, and watch the grass grow. But he was too keen and in too much of a hurry to heed the advice.

'Why do you rush, speed, and hurry so?' his teacher asked.

'I am after enlightenment,' said Brother Daniel.

His teacher smiled. 'When will you get there?'

'Oh, one more prayer perhaps, my next meditation hopefully, or an act of service maybe,' replied Brother Daniel.

'Why are you so sure enlightenment is running on ahead of you?' asked his teacher. 'Perhaps if you stood still awhile, you would find that enlightenment is here right now – but you are too busy running away from it!'

In this story, the monastery is a symbol for your mind; the teacher is a symbol for your unconditioned Self, or spirit, which is always smiling; and Brother Daniel is a symbol of your conditioned self, or ego. The unconditioned Self experiences wholeness, while the conditioned self searches for wholeness.

Much has been written about the ego, or conditioned self. The term *the ego* can be misleading, for when we say it, it sounds as if we're talking about a person, a child, or something real. Essentially put, the ego is a 'small idea' about your individual self. And the idea *is:* Everything Good is Outside. So conditioned and convinced are we by this frightening thought that we chase the world, just like Brother Daniel, searching for success, happiness, love, and peace of mind. And we dare not look within ourselves, for what if all we find is nothing, or, worse still, something rotten?

I remember once reading, although I'm not sure where now, that the word *ego* also stands for Edging God Out. This is a similar idea to Everything Good is Outside. Your conditioned self is acting on information that something is missing inside you, and that you have to search outside of yourself to find it. This thought of lack, of *not being enough,* is very frightening; and it leaves us needy, disoriented, and chasing shadows.

The ego is fear. It is also the denial of inner happiness. The ego's prayer, therefore, is always *Look out!*

'Look out, look out!' cries the ego, but the ego is blind because it doesn't believe. It looks but never finds; it asks but doesn't receive. In effect . . .

the ego is like a thirsty fish – it is confused!

Imagine a thirsty fish – a fish dying of thirst that is born in water, made of water, and surrounded by water! Just because the fish refuses to drink doesn't mean there *isn't* any water. Another analogy is to think of the ego as a bird flying high, trying to reach the sky, while all the time being *in* the sky. And a final analogy would be to think of the ego as a sparkle in a diamond while insisting there *is* no diamond.

The ego is a doubt that you are whole—that is, your conditioned self doubts that there even *is* an unconditioned Self. The unconditioned Self declares: 'I am whole,' but the conditioned self asks, 'Am I whole?' as I've shown below in Figure 1. This doubt in your essential goodness, your essential beauty, and essential wholeness is where all your pain and suffering stems from.

I AM WHOLE	AM I WHOLE?
Unconditioned	conditioned
Self	self

Our unconditioned Self is forgotten but not entirely lost as we roam the world. Every now and then we catch its fragrance, its melody, its taste. In childhood we're told stories, the significance of which hits us much later on. For instance, Hans Christian Andersen's tale *The Ugly Duckling* is a wonderful description of the ego (the duckling) and the spirit (the swan). What is the ego other than a mistaken identity?

Just like the ugly duckling, we're afraid we're not good enough, wrong, bad, and nothing; and just like the ugly duckling, we'll eventually learn that this isn't true.

Sleeping Beauty is a tale that encourages us to wake up to our inner beauty—that is, our unconditioned Self. *Beauty and the Beast* shows us how love (beauty) can help us transform our ego-thinking (beast). *Peter Pan* beckons us to remember, to imagine, and to fly free again. Pick any children's tale—*Aladdin*, *The Lion King*, and *Pinocchio*, for instance; and we're told of a spiritual journey that moves from ego to Self, fear to love, pain to joy.

One final thought about our conditioning: *It's all made up!* It has been made up, and it isn't true. What you think about yourself and what other people have told you about you is just an opinion, not a fact. It is helpful, therefore, to remember that the ego is just a thought, a thought of limitation, *that is not true.* The final verdict of the ego is that it's a mistake. It offers a small, poor, dull, limited likeness—a bad snapshot that doesn't capture the real you. In other words, *the ego is not real.*

Michelangelo, God, and Miracles

When the renowned Italian artist Michelangelo was asked by an admirer: 'How do you create your beautiful sculptures?' he gave a reply that became famous and is still told around the world to this day: 'The beauty is already there, my friend. I do not create beauty; God creates beauty. I merely chip away the surrounding marble so as to reveal the beauty. The beauty is already within. It is already perfectly in place.'

The surrounding marble Michelangelo refers to is like our conditioning; and the beauty already within the marble is like our true, unconditioned Self.

My friend Avanti encouraged me to read poetry whenever I could, particularly the metaphysical poets such as William Wordsworth, William Blake, and Robert Browning; and also the Indian poet Rabindranath Tagore and the Sufi bard Rumi, to name just a few. In one of Robert Browning's works, he refers to our 'imprisoned splendour' in much the same way that Michelangelo talks of the beauty already within the marble. He writes:

> Truth is within ourselves, it takes no rise
> From outward things, whatever you may believe.
> There is an inner centre in us all
> Where truth abides in fullness; and around
> Wall upon wall the gross flesh hems it in
> That perfect, clear perception which is Truth.
> A baffling and perverting carnal mesh
> Binds all and makes all error, but to know
> Rather consists in finding out a way
> For the imprisoned splendour to escape
> Than in achieving entry for a light
> Supposed to be without.

Alongside Avanti's tutoring, I also began to investigate schools of psychology and psychotherapy that aren't so well covered in university syllabi. My research showed me that since the end of World War II, in particular, many new schools have emerged that go way beyond Sigmund Freud and Behaviorism in their definition of what it means to be human. Freud, particularly, maintained that humans have two basic drives, *sex* and *aggression,* and that our goal in life is to be as sexy and as aggressive as politely possible. There was no higher Self, according to Freud.

The idea of a higher, spiritual, unconditioned Self is now reemerging. More and more schools of psychology now see that healing is about outgrowing your limited self-concept of the ego to embrace your true Self, one that is not conditioned or altered in any way by the world (see Table B). The terminology varies from school to school, but the basic principles and understanding are very similar.

Table B

Psychologist	School	Ego	Spirit
Alfred Adler	Individual Psychology	Guiding Fiction	Creative Self
Carl Jung	Analytical Psychology	Persona	Self
Fritz Perls	Gestalt Therapy	Self-image	Self
Roberto Assagioli	Psychosynthesis	Sub-personalities	I
R. D. Laing	Primal Integration Therapy	False Self	Real Self
Janov	Primal Integration Therapy	Unreal Self	Real Self
Eric Berne	Transactional Analysis	Adapted Child	Free Child
Dr. J. L. Moreno	Psychodrama	Conserved Roles	Spontaneity

An increasing number of psychologists are changing their minds about the limited models and concepts that have so governed human understanding. It is of interest to note that even Freud changed his mind about many of his ideas toward the end of his life. In one of my books, *Stress Busters,* I quote from Freud, who just before he died wrote: 'In the final analysis, we must love in order not to fall ill.' Psychology is finding its soul once more. And now all that remains, it seems, is for us to change our minds about ourselves.

I also became absorbed in Eastern philosophy, with its rich, vibrant, and poetic vision. Although many of these authors describe the unconditioned Self using mystical images and deeply spiritual metaphors, they are at pains to point out that an experience of this whole Self is a natural, normal, commonplace, everyday possibility. The Buddhist term *satori,* for instance, refers to instant enlightenment, *available for all and to all.*

I found the works of Sri Ramakrishna, a 19th-century mystic, to be particularly fascinating. Every word seemed strangely familiar to me. He wrote extensively about the unconditioned Self, which he referred to as the Divine Self. In one passage, he explains:

Know thyself, and thou shalt then know the non-self and the Lord of All. What is my ego? Is it my hand, or foot, or flesh, or blood, or muscle, or tendon? Ponder deep, and thou shalt know that there is no such thing as I. As by continually peeling off the skin of the onion, so by analysing the ego it will be found that there is not any real entity corresponding to the ego. The ultimate result of all such analysis is God. When egoism drops away, Divinity manifests Itself.

Over and over during my search for greater understanding, I felt I was being pulled along by a golden thread of teaching that made a connection between the unconditioned Self and God within: 'Search not in distant skies; in man's own heart God lies,' said one Japanese text. In the holy book of the Sikhs, *The Granth*, it is written: 'God is in thy heart, yet thou searchest for him in the wilderness.'

In the Psalms, it is written: 'You too are gods, sons of the most High, all of you.' Jesus tells us in the Bible: 'Ye are Gods.' Islam purports: 'Those who know themselves know their God.' And in Buddhism, it is written: 'Look within, you are the Buddha.'

The god I first learned about as a child was like a huge inflated ego, living in the sky. He was very jealous, sported a long beard, was middle-aged, had an anger problem, and was very aloof. This god blessed bombs, fixed football games, found you parking spaces, and helped you win the lottery. It was a special god that loved and hated some people more than others.

This ego-sized god apparently needs and enjoys sacrifices of live animals and young babies; and has a penchant for tobacco, drugs, and beer. It is obviously a god of fear; and therefore, a god of punishment, attack, vengeance, and judgement. Clearly . . .

great unhappiness is caused by our
misperceptions of our Self and God.

Slowly but surely, with the help of Avanti and many other teachers and mentors I met along my spiritual path, I began to heal my misperceptions of my Self and of God. Layer by layer I let go of my conditioning. It's enough to say here that I now relate to God as pure, unconditional love; and that I now see no difference between unconditional love and the unconditioned Self.

It was approximately nine years after meeting Avanti that I sat down together with my first wife, Miranda, to read a book called *A Course in Miracles,* which changed my life forever. It is a remarkable work that offers spiritual psychology training as it transforms our fearful thoughts into loving thoughts, and in giving up our ego for our real unconditional Self.

I didn't really appreciate this book at first. It was so big – bigger than Leo Tolstoy's *War and Peace* – more than 1,200 pages long, and full of religious metaphor. If truth be known, Miranda and I had both bought this book long before we met each other, and it had sat on both our shelves idle for five years! Every time I'd tried to read it, my eyes would glaze over and I'd soon be asleep, no matter what the time of day.

Other than being a great remedy for insomnia, I discovered that the *Course* had other uses, too. It made an excellent doorstop, for instance, a great paperweight, and, most important, it looked very impressive on the bookshelf. Finally, one day, Miranda and I returned to the *Course,* opened a page at random, and began to read.

The words we read were: 'The self you made [the ego] is not the Son of God [your unconditioned Self].' This message is repeated many, many times throughout the entire book. Later, there is a meditation that reads:

My true Identity is so secure, so lofty, sinless, glorious
and great, wholly beneficent and free from guilt,
that Heaven looks to It to give it light. It lights
the world as well. It is the gift my Father gave to me;
the one as well I give the world. There is no gift
but This that can be either given or received. This
is reality, and only This. This is illusion's end. It is
the truth.

    My Name, O Father, still is known to You. I have
forgotten it, and do not know where I am going, who
I am, or what it is I do. Remind me, Father, now,
for I am weary of the world I see. Reveal what You
would have me see instead.

A Course in Miracles is a constant affirmation that you are created by an unconditional thought of love that appears to have lost itself in a world of fear. Freedom, joy, and peace of mind are yours again when you remember and reconnect to your unconditioned Self. As the book says: 'Salvation requires the acceptance of but one thought; you are as God created you, not what you made of yourself.'

Choosing to Remember or to Forget

You are, in any given moment, either remembering or forgetting about your unconditioned Self, your true spiritual identity. Nothing else is really happening. When you remember that you're free, you feel happy, hopeful, trusting, generous, loving, and, above all, safe. When you doubt, however, and you forget the truth about yourself, you become afraid, isolated, and desperate; you go it alone; you protect and defend; you strive and you attack.

Perhaps you know this famous passage by William Wordsworth:

Our birth is but a sleep and a forgetting:
The soul that rises with us, our life's Star,
Hath had elsewhere its setting,
And cometh from afar:
Not in entire forgetfulness,
And not in utter nakedness,
But trailing clouds of glory do we come
From God, who is our home:
Heaven lies about us in our infancy!
Shades of the prison-house begin to close

Upon the growing Boy,
But He beholds the light, and whence it flows,
He sees it in his joy;
The Youth, who daily farther from the east
Must travel, still is Nature's Priest
and by the vision splendid
Is on his way attended;
At length the Man perceives it die away,
And fade into the light of common day.

Unhappiness is a symptom of forgetfulness, as much as joy is a symptom of remembering. When we're unhappy, balance gives way, perspective collapses, faith falters, communication often breaks down, doubt doubles, panic ensues, and a thousand different symptoms spill all around us. The disharmony we feel is ultimately a disharmony with our self. We've stepped out of our center; and we 'lose heart,' 'lose spirit,' and lose our Self.

Healing is remembering. It is what author Marianne Williamson calls 'a return to love.' Much of my therapeutic work with clients is, therefore, about helping people to rediscover the *trailing clouds of glory* within. We talk, we meditate, we laugh, we cry, we pray, we sing, we dance . . . we do whatever is necessary to help us remember the truth and let go of the pain.

At my seminars hosted by The Happiness Project, I occasionally share a poem of mine that helps me remember what my own healing and my own work is all about. It reads:

There once was a moment,
a mad, forgetful moment, that slipped
past eternity into time.
And in that moment, mad and
forgetful as it was, out of nowhere
an entire world, separate from God,
was dreamed up.
And although it was only a moment,
it felt like forever.
And although it was only a dream,
it felt so real.
In this mad, forgetful world, the
Ocean prayed to God,
'Give me water. I want water.'
The Sun, brilliant and bright, would
pray, 'Dear God, fill me with light.'
And the mighty, powerful, roaming Wind
would plea, 'Set me free, set me free.'
One time, all of sudden, and I don't quite
know why, the Silence began to speak,
'God grant me peace, grant me peace.'
Then, Peace Itself, fell to its knees,
'Dear God, please, what can I do to be
more peaceful?'
Now, looking quite perplexed, prayed,
'Dear God, what next?'
Even Eternity began to pray,
'I want to last forever and ever and ever.'
Infinity felt small,

'Dear God, help me to grow.'
And Life itself, began to cry,
'I don't ever want to die!'
And You and I, who are the essence of Love,
we cried out for love,
'God please love me,' we prayed.
'God, fill me with love,' we prayed.
'God, grant me love.'
Mad and forgetful as it was, that moment
in time soon slipped, tripped, and fell
away back into eternity.
It's all over now, save the memory –
a mad, forgetful memory, it too ready
for eternity.

In the Buddhist scripture, The Dhammapada, there is the famous 'Eight Fold Path,' which refers to eight spiritual freedoms, one of which is *right remembrance,* or right mindfulness. Disciples of Buddhism are called upon to 'Arise! Watch. Remember and forget not.' In a similar way, Jesus asked us to 'watch and pray.' To be happy, it's good to make a point of knowing what it is in your life that helps you remember truth. What is it that helps you to love, to be real, to be free? What is it that helps you wake up from the slumber of your conditioning? As for myself, I love the sounds of laughter and friendship. I love to look at the stars, to walk in nature, to listen to the river's song, to smell the heavenly scent of stargazer lilies, to watch a roaring fire, to feel its warmth and see its light. I love to be still, to smile, to meditate, and to pray. How about you?

It's important to remember what helps you to remember! For I guarantee that the next time you're ill or unhappy, you will move away from everything that supports you, strengthens you, and inspires you. Indeed, you must have already moved away or you wouldn't be so unhappy. How curious it is that we abandon our greatest sources of strength when we're stressed or challenged in some way. We tell ourselves: 'First I must work my problems out,' and only then will we ask for help.

Remembering to remember now is the key!

For four years I worked with the BBC as a counselor and executive coach. There was a church opposite the main building that had a prominent sign outside that never changed in all the time I was there. The sign read: O GOD, SHOW ME WHAT IS WRONG WITH ME. This was, I imagine, a call to worship. It often struck me that this church needed a new marketing manager!

I was once introduced to a truly beautiful prayer, the exact opposite of this church sign, which I believe offers a perfect example of how to remember and reconnect to our true, unconditioned Self. It's a prayer by a woman named Macrina Wiederkehr, and it reads:

> O God, help me to believe the truth about myself,
> no matter how beautiful it is.
> Amen.

This is real prayer. Try it. Give yourself seven days. Say this prayer each day, first thing in the morning, and then sit and listen for guidance. This prayer offers a wonderful frame of mind for remembering and reconnecting to your unconditioned Self. As you take hope into your silence, you will surely draw hope from that silence. Try this prayer for a week and you'll see what I mean.

Seeing the Light!

First, you believe, and then you see the Light.
Next, you go toward the Light. Soon, you
are in the Light. Now you are the Light.

Paul was a self-made multimillionaire. He told me so the first time we met. He talked and I listened. He told me about his wife, his life, his work, and, most of all, his children. 'I have three children I love more than anything,' he said. 'I want to give them everything I didn't have when I grew up. I tell them constantly that they can be what they want. I encourage them to strive, to work hard, to give everything every effort, to be the best they can. I always remind them they can do better, they can give more, they can be more – there are no limits.'

I listened to Paul talk about his children for almost 30 minutes. Eventually, I asked: 'Paul, what are you trying to tell me?'

He paused for a moment and bowed his head. His bullish confidence and upbeat mood vanished. I think

I even saw a tear. 'The problem is,' he said, 'my children hate me. I've given them everything, and they hate me.'

'Have you ever told your children that they are wonderful, right now, just the way they are?' I asked him. He obviously had not. 'Paul, your children don't need to be told how great they're *going* to be; what they really need is to be told how loved and how wonderful they are *now*,' I said. I also suggested that by telling his children how wonderful he thinks they are *now* he was also investing wisely in their future.

Paul had only one hesitation: 'What if I tell them they're complete and whole as you say and then they get complacent?!' We explored this common fear for a while.

'Would you have become complacent if your father had ever once told you he loved you?' I asked.

'Certainly not,' said Paul.

'Well, you have your answer then. See the Light in your children now, Paul. See the Light in them, for their sake and yours. Trust in their Light, for their sake and yours. *See* the Light,' I said.

As a psychologist, I had originally been trained to be a problem spotter. In fact, initially, I prided myself on how good I was at being able to spot people's weaknesses, neuroses, fears, and hang-ups. You see, I wanted to be a really good psychologist; and, as you probably know, a really good psychologist is someone who can always find more wrong with you than an average psychologist can!

My original training, therefore, involved: (1) spotting the problem you had that you were going to tell me about; (2) spotting the problem you had that you were *not* going to tell me about; and (3) spotting the problem you had that you didn't even know about yet! That's how creative psychology can be – you come in with a few minor problems and you leave with some major ones!

Over time, I began to have a change of heart. I started to realize that the greatest psychotherapy of all is not in pointing out people's problems and failures, but rather, in pointing people toward their Light. You see, I really do believe now that . . .

> a true healer helps you to remember and
> reconnect consciously with your inner Light.

By 'Light,' I mean your innate unconditional potential to be happy, to be loving, to be free of fear, and to be creative beyond your greatest imagination. You can never really lose your Light because your Light is *you* – your unconditioned Self – but you can forget about it. This Light feels so real when you're happy, and so unreal when you're unhappy. Hence, the pain, the fear, the loneliness, and the grief of unhappiness. When in darkness, we wonder if we will ever see the Light again.

I can remember the exact day when I first realized the absolute necessity of being able to see the Light of the unconditioned Self in healing. I was at my Stress Busters Clinic, a clinic I'd been running through the National Health Service in West Birmingham (in the U.K.) for a couple of years. I looked out on a sea of people who'd gathered for another two-hour session. This time I didn't actually see people, though. All I saw was a group of alcoholics, depressives, heart-attack victims, cancer sufferers, drug addicts, AIDS victims, people suffering phobias, and one schizophrenic.

At first I felt a wave of absolute hopelessness. I remember thinking, *How can I help all these people – their problems are so huge and so completely different from one another?!* It occurred to me that what I really needed to do was set up an individual clinic for each illness – a clinic for depression, for anxiety, and so on. Before I could really panic, I instinctively said a quick prayer: '*Dear God, help me to see this differently.*' Then, in true British fashion, I had a sip of tea. As I opened my mouth to speak, I quickly shut it again before any words could spill out. My mind was on to something. A new idea was formulating, coming through like a fax or e-mail.

I had another sip of tea while the downloading continued. It dawned on me that although these people's illnesses certainly appeared very different, they were in fact all symptoms of one single illness. Essentially put, these people were ill because they were unhappy. Each of them had somehow become unhinged from the happiness of their *unconditioned Self*. I realized, therefore, that they had come to the clinic not just to de-stress, but to remember and reconnect to happiness. They had come to see the Light.

Years earlier I'd read the works of the Greek philosopher Pythagoras, who had said: 'There is no illness, only ignorance.' Now, at last, I was beginning to see that maybe the ignorance he was referring to was the forgetting and separating from the Light of our unconditioned Self. I also began to see that my work at Stress Busters was probably, like the Tower of Pisa, slightly offcenter.

Until that time, the emphasis of my work had been, like my psychology training, problem oriented. I had spent days studying every illness, dis-ease, and stress-related problem I could find. And, although I'd mentioned happiness many times, I had never given a workshop specifically on that topic. The same was true for love, for peace of mind, for success, and for joy. Now it occurred to me that if these people could remember how to be happy again, maybe they would experience less dis-ease, and they would also handle their challenges in a much more healthy and wise way.

Sometime later, I wrote in my daily journal some words that I still call upon to this day for inspiration. They read:

Know Love; no fear
Know Joy; no pain
Know Light; no darkness
Know Wholeness; no dis-ease

Know Now; no past
Know Truth; no lies
Know God; no separation
Know Self; no other

True healers take into account any type of darkness, but their real task is to see the Light in their clients so as to help them remember and consciously reconnect to their own inner Light. In this way, both healer and client are healed together. Parenting is the same. The ultimate gift of a parent to a child is to care for the inner Light of children until they can care for it themselves. True friends are those who believe in you through thick and thin. They still see the Light in you even when your moods and behavior are dark and low. Mentors, managers, leaders, visionaries, peacemakers, and everyone who truly serves . . . they all see the Light.

rohini singh

HAPPINESS: AN ELUSIVE BUTTERFLY?

Once you begin to understand and do not let Ego get away with its manipulations you are taking the first few steps to true happiness. A happiness that does not depend on the occurrence of any outer circumstances or conditions. That just is. Within.

A MAGNET QUOTING THE FAMOUS AMERICAN AUTHOR Henry David Thoreau on the door of my refrigerator says:

> Happiness is like a butterfly: the more you chase it, the more it will elude you. But if you turn your attention to other things, it will come and sit quietly on your shoulder….

As it often happens with things that become familiar, I had stopped seeing it. The magnet, I mean. When asked to write an essay on Happiness for this anthology, I began to contemplate the quotation. It seems contradictory, does it not? Everyone seems to be in the pursuit of this preferred state called happiness. And there are many paths, parameters and possibilities that can help one attain it. It certainly seems to be something that has to be worked towards. Self-help books fill the shelves of book stores, each offering their own secret formula. Workshops teaching tools and techniques promise that *that* is how you will go away feeling if you diligently do what is taught to you. Manifest it, attract it, intend it, and it will be yours. It is a *goal*. Something we are chasing?

It is inextricably tied up with other parameters too. After all, if we don't achieve 'success' at work, in relationships, with reference to our wishes, desires and dreams, how can one hope to be happy? I contemplate the magnet on my fridge door. The more you chase it, the more it will elude you . . . it is confusing. Have we all not been taught that working hard, reaching goals, fulfilling desires is what will make you happy, at peace, purposeful? When they are attained, ofcourse. Then you set about making new lists, setting higher parameters, challenging yourself still further, pushing comfort zones to climb higher on the ladder of achievement. In fact, it seems to be an almost automatic process. No sooner do you 'reach' a much looked-forward-to dream, there is hardly a moment to pause and relax, when the 'next step' suggests itself. You are filled with fresh enthusiasm, the zest of pursuing a new venture. It gives you a high, drives you; makes the adrenaline pump as unforeseen circumstances, uncertainty and risk raise their heads. They are the counterpoints, the 'friction' that makes the whole game worthwhile. That allows you to feel a sense of achievement when you 'reach.'

That enhances the happiness quotient, perhaps? The more impossible the goal seems at the start, the more satisfaction it gives at the end. Often, it seems like a carrot, always dangling just a little out of reach. Luring you with promises of more, baiting you, enticing you to keep following it.

If you stop and look back at your journey, surely there would have been times when you felt supremely happy. It must have been the times when something you had dreamt about, became a reality. Every life has milestones, markers along the journey. Times of celebration. A birth. A graduation. A marriage. A festival. A promotion. An award. You feel happy when things go 'your way'. The way you have envisioned.

When they don't – you lose someone beloved to you; a child follows a path you do not approve of; a relationship fails; someone betrays your trust; a business suffers – there is suffering. You feel unhappy and let down. By others, and at a deeper level, by Life, and even God. One thing is for sure. Happiness is not a permanent state. It is one we are all seeking, but it is ephemeral. In fact, we have been warned, in the early years of childhood, not to 'laugh too much or too hard, because otherwise we will soon be crying.' Happiness cannot be trusted to stay, is the metaphorical message.

Is it this impermanent, untrustworthy, elusive quality, Thoreau's butterfly, that we are all hoping to 'capture'? Is it a trap?

To ask this question is itself a moment of grace. Most of us never question this direction: towards happiness/away from whatever causes discomfort. There are two ways we may pause to contemplate it. We lose everything; all the parameters that made us happy and perhaps then, in the midst of the misery, we question whether that is all there is to life. Or, which may seem a little more surprising, we ask the same question when we 'have it all.' We have achieved all we set ourselves out to; the goals have been reached; everything is as we desired and yet, what is that small voice of restlessness, of unease which points to an internal emptiness in the external fullness. It urges you to contemplate; to rearrange, to rethink. It can be a turning point that upturns the way you have been viewing your Life's journey.

The question that may suggest itself is 'Can anything external make you truly happy?' Well, it does, of course, would be the immediate answer, but not for too long. In fact , anxiety about how long it will stay, is the first cause of its disappearance! Trying to hold on to it, makes it elusive. We are human and programmed to want more of what is pleasurable and happiness is a pleasurable state. Hence it hooks us. Akin to an itch, the more you scratch, the more you need to.

Apart from wished for circumstances, however, there are other things that make us happy. Beauty, whether you create it, or observe it, makes one happy. Listening to a beautiful piece of music, watching the sun rise, a flower bloom, a child smile, are all special moments that evoke something deep within us. And they lie outside. But how they make you feel is hard to describe, is it not? And therein lies a clue to their power. They are inexpressible because they take you *beyond the mind*. Where? Though using the senses, they pull you back to a deep space within. Even a few minutes of being in that space is inexplicably refreshing, rejuvenating, relaxing.

There are different kinds of happiness then! Some lie outside and it becomes increasingly clear that they can never make you happy in any permanent way. In fact, when you contemplate it deeper you realize that it is a mistake in the first place to expect your 'goals', circumstances or even relationships to bring you any kind of lasting fulfillment. But there are other beauty-full moments that point to an experience of complete happiness. For no reason. It is hard for the mind to understand that this could be so but at some time or other each of us has experienced it and know it to be true.

What is the source of *this* unconditional happiness? This happiness that lies within. It needs no-thing to make it complete. It is not something to be striven for or reached. It is already present, the Essence of who you truly are. It does not need anything to happen to allow you to feel it. It lies not in hectic activity, plans or performances. It is found most easily in silence. It requires you not to do but to **be**. It is not a transient, flitting conditional quality but a *state*. It is what you experience when you are centered, in flow and alignment with life. In the present moment.

All spiritual traditions and masters hint at it. One of the world's greatest poets, Kabir tells the deer not to go searching for musk. It lies within. A beautiful story, narrated in different versions in different traditions tells of a woman searching under a lamp outside her house for a key. A passer by asks her what she is doing and on being told, in an attempt to help her, advises:

'Why don't you try to remember where you
  dropped it?'
'Oh I know that,' she replies, 'I dropped it inside
  the house!'
Surprised by her answer, the passer by then queries:
  'Then why are you looking for it outside?'
'Because this is where the light is!' she answers.

It is the same with our pursuit of happiness. We are looking in the wrong place.

WHERE SHOULD WE LOOK THEN AND HOW?

It might be easier to answer the question if we reflect on what makes us unhappy. The answer is quite obvious. When things do not go the way we wish, we feel uncomfortable. We suffer. If we look at this phenomenon more closely it is quite clear to see that *when we resist what is, we suffer.* A deeper reflection reveals that it is not so much the prevalent circumstance that is the cause of our misery, but our 'fight' with it. Our questioning about 'how could this happen to me' or 'why is this happening' is what causes the pain. Our wanting things to be different. The minute you drop this desire, peace prevails. The circumstance does not vanish or change of course, but you allow Life to unfold exactly as it is and when you are really able to surrender and step back, you realize that it is all perfect exactly as it is.

Is this not a passive, resigned stance, you may question. Actually it is the opposite. It is not devoid of 'action' as it seems on the face of it. It is the way of intelligent, intuitive response. Metaphorically, if it rains, and you wish to stay dry, you respond by taking out your umbrella. If you wish to get wet, you don't! If it is hot, you do what you need to keep cool and the opposite in winter. You don't waste energy questioning or complaining about the weather. You do not try to stop the rain. It is the same with the weather of Life. Sometimes it is sunny, at other times, rainy. At still other times, it is stormy and turbulent. All phases pass and all are part of an organic rhythmic ebb and flow. Acceptance of things as they are is the only way to this portal of true happiness, if one can call it that. More accurately, what reason can there be for unhappiness if there is a deep, trusting and joyful acceptance of what is?

What stands in the way? The Ego. The conditioned you. The composite personality structure with its likes, dislikes, desires, fears, and it's own ideas about how things should be. It is who you *think* you are. Far from being You, it is merely a sense of separation that has developed as you grew, alienating you from others, and binding you into a contracted 'me-ness'. The stronger it has become, the more you struggle. The more 'do-ership' there is in your actions, the higher is the wall of isolation. The more you live in fear and the more you struggle to make things happen in the only way you think is 'right': your way. The only way. But that is not how Life may flow. Every time it doesn't , it is a set up for unnecessary unhappiness and misery. Leave alone your appreciating the 'gift' that lies hidden in the 'adversity', you cannot even see everything that is still in place because the one circumstance that, in your opinion, is not, consumes your attention. It is an Ego trap.

The Ego is anti-happiness. Whenever it sees you slipping into a state of ease and peacefulness, it is apt to churn up things to get you back in its control. It has a whole file of things from the past that it can use to hook you. Regrets, guilt, sadness, shame, are part of its weaponry. If it does not succeed with them, it can always turn to the future with its inbuilt uncertainties, to blindfold you with fear and anxiety. It can keep you away from being happy and problem free in the present moment with one or other tactic. It is only in the present moment that it has no place or access to you.

The only way out is recognition of these games that the Ego plays. Once you begin to understand and do not let Ego get away with its manipulations you are taking the first few steps to true happiness. A happiness that does not depend on the occurrence of any outer circumstances or conditions. That just is. Within.

If one does not gain access to this 'well' of inner happiness, in actuality, nothing outside can ever 'make' you happy. And if you have discovered this inner place of joy, nothing outside can make you unhappy. In fact, everything, no matter how ordinary, becomes extraordinary.

The end of the journey is total surrender. Is it defeatist? No. It is a result of life time of evolution. Is it easy? No. It is not because you are habitually in the grip of the Ego and the Ego does not support surrender. Surrender would mean the death of the Ego. When it does happen, and you cannot make it, it is the simplest, most innocent way to live. Fear is replaced by faith. Struggle is replaced with peace and trust. Resistance is replaced by flow.

Imagine a leaf that falls into a river. It allows itself to be carried. Splashed over rocks, spun around in whirlpools, thrown out onto the shore, taken back in, it 'reaches' it's destination, whatever and wherever that might be.

Being like that leaf is the only way to be truly happy. Dropping your will and flowing with the river of life. Supported by it, guided by it, and enjoying every moment of the adventure!

Allowing the butterfly to come and sit softly on your shoulder ....

shobhaa dé

HAPPINESS HAPPENS TO THOSE
WHO SEEK IT

...we should be looking no further than within our own hearts. God is an emotion. Life is God. Cherish life and you will find God. When you find God, happiness will find you!

L ET ME GIVE YOU THE GOOD NEWS FIRST: IT IS POSSIBLE to be happy. Yes, even in today's times, when the odds are stacked so heavily against happiness.

However, I must warn you that there is a catch to being happy. And it is this: In order to achieve happiness, a person first has to want to be happy. Desire it. Identify it. And acknowledge as much. When was the last time you – yes, you – thought about being happy? Actually sat down and said to yourself: 'I want to be happy.' Sounds simple? Foolish? Think about it…

I did. And this very elementary statement of a very fundamental desire, made me acutely aware of my own state of mind at that point (restless, irritable, intolerant). Once I'd identified the basics (happiness-generators), I then went about discarding most of the causes that stood in the way of my achieving this really, really underrated condition that we take so much for granted but barely understand. We assume everybody else in the world is happy but us. We also assume, everybody's idea of happiness is more or less the same as our own. We focus excessively on things that don't make us happy, rather than on those that do. It becomes a vicious cycle of regurgitating all that annoys, rather than a remembrance of all the uplifts. Some years back, I noticed that I had started to frown more and smile less! How awful … that's when I said to myself: 'It's time to take stock… starting now!'

But first, I had to regress…become a child again. Or rather, rediscover the child in me -- the little girl who used to laugh a lot, often for no apparent reason. The same girl, who possessed an insatiable curiousity about nearly every aspect of everyday life. The pony-tailed teenager who'd rush out of the house to dance in the rain, and talk to the moon because it was smiling. When was the last time I'd stopped to stare with fascination at a particularly pretty autumn leaf…a painting…or listen to snatches of a long forgotten song? Today, I'm fortunate enough to have the resources to buy some of the things I used to dream about owning as a young person. But do I have the time to enjoy them? I glance at my pricey wrist watch and realize it just sits on my wrist as the hours fly… I've stopped noticing its classic lines and sophisticated mechanism. Imagine the irony of it all.

We spend years lusting after material objects that are supposed to enhance our lives in tangible ways, but in reality, by the time we acquire these goodies and revel in our well-earned lifestyle perks, we are either too blasé, too exhausted or... this is the worst... too ill to appreciate our good luck! That's when reality checks kick in. For a lot of prosperous men, the trappings of success (multiple cars, great homes, impressive whiskies on the bar, rare cognacs, Cuban cigars, a choice of young bed partners...) oh, all that they may have fantasized about during their lean and mean youth - it's right there, waiting to be devoured. Damn. If only the by-pass surgery hadn't taken the fun out of the promised adventure. Imagine... a single stroke of a pen on a cheque can change ones life as drastically as an entirely different kind of medical stroke that can kill in an instant, too.

Sometimes, when I'm feeling especially philosophical, I transport myself mentally to my adored beach in Goa. I recall all those magical moments, lying on a deck chair, feeding papayas to stray cows, snoozing lazily, sipping chilled coconut water, reading in a desultory fashion and enjoying the warmth of a winter sun on my bare shoulders. Later, much later, while locating my flip-flops half-buried in the sand, a strange realization shakes me out of my temporary stupor. It's the sand that does it... all those millions of tiny grains, only to be impatiently shaken off. I look down at my toes and laugh. One day, I too shall be reduced to less than that grain of sand. So shall we all. How foolish and worthless our vanities appear in such a chilling context. I promptly straighten my shoulders and look skywards...same story. In this vast and mysterious universe, who and what are we? Not even the tiniest of tiny specks. It is such a liberating moment…. I generally throw my head back and laugh at the absurdity of existence. For a few days that follow, I follow my heart, not head. It's reassuring to know that's still possible. I listen to plaintive Goan mandos and feel deliciously emotional. Charlie Brown was so right when he declared: 'Happiness is a sad song…'

What is it that makes my heart soar?

Topping it is 'Family'. I guess 99 per cent of the people in the world would readily agree. No family, no joy. In India, we still believe in the deeply nurturing aspects of a fulfilling family life. We continue to value the concept of 'Kutumb'. It is where we seek our deepest emotions… it is where we retreat when we need comfort. I cannot think of happiness without the love and warmth that family provides. Starting there, I'd like to share my 25 key tips for finding (and keeping) the universe's most elusive, most desired emotional state – happiness. These basic, uncomplicated guidelines have helped me. At least a few of them are bound to help you. For, as a stressed out banker-friend trustingly asked me: 'At the end of the day, every human being wants just one thing – to be happy. Right?'

Yup. Absolutely right!

1. *Learn to Let Go*

Easier said than done. But it is possible. Baggage weighs you down, makes you miserable. What's the point of going over the minutae of a relationship that has soured? It could be with a spouse, lover or a business associate. Once it's over, it's over. Move on. Take your time to come to terms with the break. But don't keep brooding once you have made the decision to part. This applies equally to a bad experience with a stranger who may have duped you. Learn from it, but discard the negative emotion generated by the memory. It serves zero purpose. The only thing that works in a break up, is a clinical incision that cuts neatly and permanently. Remember, sutures heal. A festering wound, oozes.

2. *Be Selfish. Be Vain*

Ask anyone: 'Do you lead a selfish life?' Or, ' Are you vain?' and the person will hotly deny it. We all like to see ourselves as generous people who help others. But in reality, most of us only help those who can help us! I have taken the best lessons out of Ayn Rand's remarkable treatise titled *The Virtues of Selfishness*. If you don't give your own self priority, if you don't look after your health, appearance and well being, you can't make anyone around you happy either. Being 'constructively selfish' is very different from being mean and self-centred. Similarly, vanity is not just about narcissism. It extends well beyond that narrow definition.

As a responsible person, you owe it to yourself to eat smart, live smart, look good. If your self image is positive, you will convey positive vibes to those around you. A frustrated, embittered person who refuses to address the issues that lead to a negative approach, will find it difficult to overcome life's many hurdles. Invest in yourself – because you are worth it!

3. *Slow Down*

I completely mean that, even if I don't adhere to it myself. I know I'm pushing the pace, I know I need to cut the speed…but I say helplessly: 'I can't!' Rubbish. There is nothing that compelling… nothing that can't be kept on hold. And yet, here I am lunatically hurtling towards some self-defined goal. What on earth for? I see countless clones around me making the same mistake. Often, I 'advise' them to take a break. But what about my own crazy schedule? The good part is I am aware of my punishing routine. Chances are, I'll fix it soon. Wish me luck!

4. *Express Gratitude*

Articulate your feelings when someone does you a good turn. Don't take it for granted that people owe it to you to be 'nice'. This is entirely untrue. Goodness and grace, especially with no strings attached, need to be recognized, at least in your own busy heart. Ideally, write the person a warm and sincere note appreciating the gesture. Pick up the phone…send a text. These are life's unexpected moments, make sure you remain tuned in to them.

5. *Listen with Your Heart, Not just Your Ears*

So often, we pretend to be listening, our ears hear the words being spoken, but our hearts are elsewhere, and nothing really registers later. What an insult to the person doing the talking. The problem for this is not a lack of interest in the other's concerns, it is a lack of time. Our attention spans have shrunk to an extent we no longer invest even a bit of our precious micro-seconds on another's situation, unless it directly impacts our own! *Matlab ki baat hai.* Cacophony has replaced conversation. Selective deafness dominates social intercourse.

6. *Teach Yourself to Trust*

Agreed the world isn't the most amazing place, but it isn't all that terrible either. These days, suspicion rules. We are constantly looking over our shoulders to see who's carrying a knife... the same one that will stab us in the back the moment our attention gets diverted. Husbands and wives play cat-and-mouse games. Siblings don't trust each other, children accuse their parents of vile acts, and parents are wary of their kids. Isn't that sad? Forget business partnerships where nobody trusts anybody. It appears as if we are all lone warriors ready to attack at the first sign of aggression. But the minute you surrender your doubts and stop being cynical, you realize just how many wonderful people there are out there, who may actually risk their own lives to save yours!

7. *Touch and Go*

Really, that's all it needs – one tiny touch before you get busy. Just that hurried physical contact with someone you care for, is enough to last several hours and offer comfort. We have stopped hugging one another... why, we rarely hug our own children. No wonder India's Hugging Saint became a world-wide phenomenon. She tapped into a vacant space and found countless takers.

Everyone needs to be hugged, stroked, embraced, cuddled, kissed, caressed. Even a pet at home demands a pat of appreciation. Imagine then what we are missing out on? Forget hugging, we no longer make direct eye contact. Isn't that sad? Make it a point to demonstrate your affection by reaching out briefly, at least once a day... it's worth the effort many times over. If nothing else works, hire a masseur for a more professional 'touch'.

8. *Stop Being a Control Freak*

Of course, we all want to stay on top of our lives and all that. But at what cost? Cardiac arrest? Hypertension? I am the first one to admit, I get disoriented if I am not in control of my time and activities. I realize it's a dumb thing to do, and am actively addressing the syndrome. I spot similar victims around me. How silly are we to think we can actually control anything! Being reasonably organized is one thing. Being obsessive about it, another. I'm striving to find the right balance. So should you.

9. *Shut Up*

That's right. Keep quiet. Not every argument needs a resolution. Life is more than a game of one upmanship. Often, there is more charm and satisfaction in holding ones peace, especially if tempers are running high. If one person backs off and stays quiet, chances are the argument itself loses steam and fizzles out. In retrospect, the whole thing looks absurd and exaggerated, anyway. So, why not be the bigger person, and back off?

10. *Have a Heart*

This is about compassion, yes. But on a more selfish level, it is about following your heart, too. If your heart isn't in what you do, walk away. You cannot succeed in either a career or a relationship that you aren't embracing – whole-heartedly. Imagine being stuck in a job or a marriage that only gives you grief! What for? As the cliché goes, life is way to short to throw it away on activities that are devoid of joy. The minute you opt for something or someone you love, you will succeed. The heart has its reasons….as Pascal wrote years ago. Listen to it…

11. *Count*

No, not just your blessings (which you should and must), but count… as in 1-2-3-4-5, before you make an important decision, or lose your temper. Believe me, counting has saved many a job and marriage! The trick is to remember to do so…on time! Counting slowly and with concentration, buys time, and that, as any skillful negotiator will tell you, ensures you have the advantage, while your opponent fumes. It's not important to win every debate. But the fragile state of your arteries? Now, that's important.

12. *Confide*

Secrecy has its uses. But so does a confession. Confidantes come with in-built risks, unless you are blessed enough to stumble upon a friend or a family elder you can trust. While it isn't all that easy to find such persons, it's worth taking a chance with someone who inspires a certain level of confidence…enough for you to get a few things off your chest, and feel lighter. In these ultra- paranoid times, we tend to keep everything bottled up, afraid that even a small slip up will be used against us by the very person(s), who has feigned sympathy and interest in the problem. Well…so be it! You win some and lose some. Betrayal can be devastating. But it's still better to seek advice by sharing those troubling problems than living with a constant feeling of being choked.

13. *Compliment People*

Why stinge on praise? Who doesn't like to be appreciated? Walk up to the person who has earned your respect, and say so. It costs nothing, but goes a long way in the long run. Never be fake in this regard, for soon you'll be found out. There's nothing more annoying than discovering a double-faced hypocrite, who lays it on when face-to-face and trashes you when your back is turned. Say it when you mean it. But say it! Recognizing someone else's gifts will make you a better person automatically.

14. *Extend Help*

If you find yourself in a situation where your intervention would lead to a positive outcome, go ahead and extend your hand. Don't walk away when you see someone in distress. Make a phone call, if nothing else. Often, summoning help (police, doctor, ambulance), can make the difference between life and death. Surely, you'll hate yourself later for not doing something when you could?

We have become far too indifferent and insular to the suffering of fellow beings – nobody wants to get 'involved'. Why not? Only cowards walk away from a crisis. Intervening in a crisis ought to be an obligation for anybody caught in such a situation. You must do whatever is needed at that point to aid the victim. Remember, it could be you, lying there bleeding on the ground while people jump over your prone body and leave you to die.

15. *Grow a Garden*

You don't need acres of space to achieve this – a small patch will do. And if even that is not available, get yourself a few hardy indoor plants. Most Indian homes keep a Tulsi on the kitchen windowsill. Apart from the traditional significance, Tulsi's medicinal properties are well-documented. Given the sensitive nature of my throat, and the high pollution levels in Mumbai, I scrupulously chew five Tulsi leaves dipped in honey, first thing in the morning. My throat has been behaving ever since I started the routine. My own little garden at home is very precious to me, and hugely therapeutic. On days when I wake up feeling blah, and I see the hibiscus in full bloom, my spirits soar at the beautiful sight. Taking care of plants makes you feel responsible for life itself. Tending rose bushes, or merely watering lucky bamboos, is an act that is strangely satisfying, especially when it yields results. I take the arrival of each new leaf of the Frangipani as a personal victory!

15. *Cry Your Eyes Out*

Go on…it's such a great feeling. There's nothing as de-stressing as a really good cry. Don't make it a habit, though. Save up those tears for something worthy. But once they start, don't stop them. We have forgotten how to cry! We have no time to shed those clogged up tears. In the process, we have let our tear ducts dry up, so when we really, really need to let go, nothing emerges from those dry, cold eyes.

I cry very easily, much to the embarrassment of my family. Why, I even cry while watching the stupidest Bollywood film. But mainly, it's music that makes me cry. And beauty. The helplessness and trust of innocent children has the same effect. As do sunsets…and the goodness of strangers.

Men suppress their tears because society doesn't endorse them. I think the world would be a far better, less aggressive place if men were to cry more than they do at present. I want to tell them, real men do –and should cry. It makes men more human. And therefore, more attractive. Let the 'kerchiefs do their job, guys – cry away. And feel happy doing so!

16. *Eat, Drink and be Merry*

Yup. But make sure you do so minus guilt. Eating each meal with enthusiasm and gusto does not make you a glutton! Food – whether it's comfort food or a gourmet meal – is the provider of elementary but immense pleasure. To remain indifferent to the everyday act of eating, is to deny yourself a great source of happiness. No matter what's on your thali, if you pay attention to it, respect the person who has cooked it, and engage yourself fully in the act of eating itself, on a very conscious level, you will automatically find yourself getting drawn into a more sensual world, experiencing something vivid and wonderful. Great food has great recall. Remember, memorable meals is a pleasure in itself.

Aaah, when it comes to drink, to each his own. If you like your alcohol, consume it sans pressure. There is no point in being a closet drinker, which can lead to clinical depression. Drink when you are in the mood, drink with people you feel comfortable with, drink if you want to celebrate. But don't drink if you think alcohol takes away sorrow. For, all it does is compound it.

As for being merry – that's easy! Good food, good wine and good company – what's your excuse?

17. *Music*

You know why it is called the balm for the soul? Because music alone has the ability to calm, soothe, heal, restore – and music asks for nothing in return, not even a 'thank you'! One of the best, most thoughtful birthday gifts I received was from my friend Gitaah (God bless her!). Being a singer and a music lover, who has frequently transported audiences through her gift (what a voice! Where does it come from?), Gitaah took the immense trouble to load over 300 of my very special songs and tracks on a dinky, little iPod, before presenting it to me with a sweet and affectionate note on a recent birthday. I was so touched, so thrilled and so moved, I couldn't stop weeping… or singing! The iPod has since become my best friend and most favoured stress-buster.

Apart from any therapeutic value it provides, the sheer, unadulterated pleasure of surrendering to music, be it Elvis Presley, Pandit Bhimsen Joshi, A. R. Rahman or Tchaikovsky, makes me feel one with the divine. It also makes me acutely aware of the fact that I had down-graded music in my silly list of priorities for way too long. I am delighted to report it is now back where it belongs – right up there with the few priceless treasures I most value. These days, listening to the most mindless Bollywood dance tracks on my priceless present, brings an instant smile to the lips…my feet start tapping and life itself appears as gaudy and unreal as the Bollywood film *Om Shanti Om*!

18. *Money Madness*

Agreed. Moolah helps. Big moolah helps hugely. But can it save a lost soul? We all need money. But do we need to chase it at the cost of all else – health, family, fun? When was the last time you stopped running after a monetary goal and said to yourself: 'To hell with that extra buck in the bank… I'm going to a movie.' Try suggesting that to a young person and see the expression of utter and total disbelief on the face: 'Are you mad? Have you lost it? The markets are opening in New York/Hong Kong/Tokyo… there's so much riding on the dollar… and you want me to miss out on a possible killing?'

But what about missing out on life? A walk in the rain? When was the last time you stopped to watch a sunset? Heard a bird sing? Admired a painting? Whistled an old, forgotten tune? In our mindless pursuit of wealth and status, we are cheating ourselves of simple, everyday pleasures that once recharged our batteries and energized us in a jiffy.

Money has become sexier than sex itself! The biggest

turn on for a generation that foolishly believes plastic makes the impossible, possible. 'Have credit card, will over-spend' is the mantra that provides all the orgasms. Soon credit cards may replace condoms. The sickness of compulsive consumerism is catching on rapidly. The only thing that can save us is reconnecting ... with one another, and our past.

19. *Learn to Lose*

It's really ok to not win every single time. And it's also ok to feel terrible when you lose. But feeling terrible and giving in to depression or feelings of low self-worth, are not the same thing. Losing with grace is an art in itself. Knowing when to quit, is another. Nobody stays ahead of the game permanently. Win some, lose some – that's how it goes. And always will. Losing to an opponent who deserves to win, is easy. But conceding defeat to a duffer can be a killer. Losing with ones dignity intact, provides a different high, and if you can achieve the feat, you emerge a stronger person.

Lose with a smile, even if at that point all you want to do is cry. I remember how devastated I felt during an inter-school athletics championship, when our relay time lost to a rival school because of a clumsy baton pass. That tiny error cost us the coveted shield. We were shattered and upset, till our games teacher told us to cheer up and smile. What about, we asked glumly. She just grinned and said: ' Because people look their best when they are able to rise above defeat.' Brilliant! Had she added to our despondency at that point by chastising us, we would have revelled in it, but by providing an inspirational message, she made us feel instantly better about ourselves. We went back the next year determined to regain the trophy – and did just that!

20. *Re-prioritise*

So you think you have it all neatly wrapped up? All loose ends tied? Every moment accounted for? You believe you are genuinely on top of your time? And on top of your life? You have, if not all, at least most of the answers. Why, you even have a 'Plan- B' in place incase the original one doesn't work out.

Well… guess what? Life has a nasty way of pulling the plug on the best laid plans. It's called the unpredictability factor. Out of the blue, disaster strikes – a mate dies, a child falls seriously sick, a sibling is diagnosed with a terminal illness, financial disaster hits you, an accident occurs…. Oh, so many ghastly things can take place without prior intimation. A plane crash, floods, fire, earthquake…. Look at what happened after the Tsunami, or 9/11 ?

Nothing ever prepares you for the far reaching consequences of unexpected crises. When questioned, so many people the world over have defined the moment that changed their perspectives permanently and made them pause, reassess – as the one when they were forced to confront death! All of them have said more or less the same thing – money, and the mad pursuit of it – was the first 'priority' to recede. What use is money in the face of tragedy… death… failing health? As our elders often say: 'No health equals no wealth'.

Money is only as important as you make it. If it enslaves you, your peace of mind is gone forever. There are times I watch wealthy people during their 'off' moments. Say, in an aircraft. I see their anxious expressions, faces crumpled up with tension, frown lines criss-crossing already furrowed foreheads. And I feel intensely sorry for their plight. I know they have brought it on themselves. They have chosen to be where they are. But at what cost? They first make millions. Then they spend millions in order to remain healthy and calm enough to enjoy those millions. Make any sense? Not to me.

Right now, young India is in the grip of Money Fever. Ask any 20-something what he/she wants to do, and the prompt response is – make money. Preferably, overnight. We worship our millionaires and billionaires. We devour news about their latest acquisitions. Corporate jets, fancy yachts… we love their lifestyle. But do we also love their life? If we look carefully behind the public mask, there is abject loneliness and sorrow. Disillusionment and defeat. So many top honchos, sick of the tyranny of their extreme lives, decide to opt out. But I genuinely believe, you don't have to head for the Himalayas in search of salvation. A successful person appreciates the value of balance in life. There is no need to run away from responsibility. To renounce. The solution does not lie in taking 'sanyas'. All you need is a periodic, good, hard look at those life-goals.

Be honest with yourself: how badly do you want that raise, new car, farm house, holiday abroad? How much are you willing to give up in order to achieve that distant goal? What about the quality of your life? Do you rest well at night? When was the last time you felt totally relaxed, without the aid of alcohol? When did you make love without keeping one eye on the clock? Are you guilty of bringing the laptop and Blackberry into the bedroom? Have play stations replaced parenting in your family? It is never about how much wealth you have – it is about what you do with it. Cardiac arrest or crores in the bank? The choice is yours.

21. *Sleep*

Sounds simple, and therefore unimportant. But do you know that women in particular, go through life in a state of serious sleep deprivation? That most of them never ever 'catch up' on lost slumber? Have you also wondered why international researchers spend so much time and money going into the intricacies of sleep disturbances these days? It's because scientists have discovered the far-reaching devastation caused by insufficient sleep...and the picture isn't looking good.

A charged up female executive I met in Delhi, told me she had turned into an insomniac due to the demanding nature of her work. She finds herself tossing and turning in bed, hours after switching off the lights: 'I can't wait for the morning… I am unable to relax…I am addicted to stress!' She claims she has tried it all – meditation, deep breathing exercises, yoga, a shot of cognac, a glass of milk, a warm bath… even boring books. Nothing works. Her mind is in overdrive, she is over wrought, and she resents the hours 'wasted' in sleep. Phew! The consequences have been terrible – she has no friends, no family life, and no leisure. She falls sick more often than she cares to admit, and any suggestion that she needs to slow down, is met with a derisive, dismissive snort.

Well, here's an admission: while listening to her story, I found several echoes in my own life. I too underestimate the healing value of sleep and tend to push myself long after the world has called it a day. I abhor afternoon siestas, even though I know how restful they are (ten years ago, I couldn't do without my post-lunch nap). I feel guilty and wretched on the rare occasions when I cat-nap. I also feel frustrated when I watch the rest of my family sleeping peacefully. Like the driven executive, I too am crippled by the thought that I'm 'wasting time' by sleeping. But at least, I am aware of my short-sightedness and plan to address it soon.

Babies and puppies look wonderful because they sleep most of the time! We have to wake up to the fact that eight hours of sleep restores us more effectively than all those multi-vits we pop. Let's learn a little from the

Latinos who eat well, drink well, sleep well… and make time for love.

22. *Dance*

Sometime back, I attended Shiamak Davar's amazing musical revue titled *I Believe*. I have watched Shiamak grow into a consummate performer over the past 25 years. But more than that, I have seen him use dance as a movement that transforms lives. It is inspirational and exhilarating to see how energetically Shiamak has spread the message of love, peace, harmony by getting everybody to get up and dance, regardless of any consideration. You don't need to be young, slim, supple, sexy or hot. You don't have to wear a leotard or make-up. You only have to get to your feet and sway to the beat. Anybody can do that – even someone with two left feet!

Shiamak's approach to dance is spiritual and uplifting, as is evident from his inclusive style of teaching. Whether the participant is in a wheel chair, or otherwise physically challenged, Shiamak designs a role that accommodates each disability, without the person feeling in the least patronized or pitied. Dance with Dignity is his message. And it works.

Free style dancing is easy… unlike classical dance forms that require training, discipline and talent. Dancing for the love of dancing, frees you from self-consciousness, even if you think you lack the grace and rhythm to move to the music. Who cares? You aren't going to be judged. And you aren't being watched. It's not *Naach Baliye* and you should tell yourself to just let go… whirl, twirl, jump and swirl. If you prefer dancing with other people, why not enroll for Dancercise classes? Sweat it out… trust me, it's far more fun than hours spent on a treadmill. Go for it… if 50 cent and hip-hop tracks do it for you, shake that leg, move those hips… shake, rattle and roll.

23. *Daan*

Charity does not begin and end with writing a fat cheque and sitting back smugly thinking you've done something commendable. Giving, in the true sense, goes beyond donating money. It involves giving of yourself. Sharing time and emotions, interests and ideas. It's about real enrichment of yourself, and others who can benefit from your experience. There is a beautiful word called 'daan', which defies accurate translation. 'Daan' is an all-encompassing act, that includes kindness and compassion, as much as donations and gifts.

Serving the less fortunate, in whichever capacity, makes you aware of your own good fortune, fills you with grace and gratitude, humility and joy. It doesn't have to be a grand gesture. Not everyone is Warren Buffet or Bill Gates – but look at their examples. Even, an everyday act of concern, a reaching out to someone who needs help is, in itself a fulfilling way of compensating for an otherwise self-centered existence. I know people who volunteer time and effort, working with cancer afflicted children, most of them terminally ill. Each hospital visit drains them completely. Yet, they go back, week after week because they know within themselves that their precious time is best served with children who have very little of that precise commodity themselves.

The world is waking up to the pure joy of giving. Some of the biggest names in entertainment, make sure they participate in programmes that support deserving causes, be it AIDS or female infanticide. The message their involvement sends out is powerful enough to motivate thousands of others globally to engage in similar movements that eventually lead to permanent change and personal transformations.

Even if you don't have the time to participate in such organizations, why not start in your own backyard? How about spending half-an-hour teaching an under-privileged child in your locality? Spreading literacy and empowering even a single person, will make a huge difference, as anybody who has done so, will tell you. The day that same child comes to meet you armed with a college degree, may turn out to be one of the most memorable days of your life.

24. *Just Do It*

Impossible is nothing. Strange, how the tag line of a world famous brand has the power to push individuals into new directions. Whether or not Nike sold more trainers with the 'Just Do It,' ad campaign is irrelevant. But so many years after it was launched, I still quote it to people who dither over decisions. There is something so compelling about the essential message – an inbuilt urgency that demands instant action.

No matter how big or small the issue, the idea is to handle it well. To optimize, to do it with all your heart. Whenever I find myself feeling demotivated, I recall the slogan and get to the task with fresh enthusiasm. It helps that I love what I do. And that's the other thing – if you don't actively love your vocation, you'll remain resentful and miserable, crippled by self-doubt and waiting to opt out. So, make sure you identify that which you enjoy more than anything else – and success is bound to follow.

25. *Embrace Life*

As the cliché goes, life is way too short to begin with. Why fight when you can love? When you embrace life unconditionally, you value each and every moment. And when each moment becomes precious enough, you derive the maximum enjoyment out of it. In that beautiful moment, you discover God. And goodness... love and laughter. Peace and beauty. Finding God has been our quest since time immemorial. We foolishly look for him in the most obvious of places – temples, churches, mosques and synagogues. On mountain tops and in the sky. When in reality, we should be looking no further than within our own hearts. God is an emotion. Life is God. Cherish life and you will find God. When you find God, happiness will find you!

Happiness happens to those who seek it.

sri sri ravi shankar

IN PURSUIT OF HAPPINESS

A wise one is happy even in difficult times and the foolish one is unhappy even in good times.

HAPPINESS IS OUR TRUE NATURE. IT IS THE STATE OF our being when there is neither stress nor want. Consciously or unconsciously, everyone is in the pursuit of happiness. The irony is that one gets stuck in the journey and seldom reaches the goal.

If happiness is linked to the fulfilment of desires or wants, then it is short lived; as one desire is fulfilled another arises, thus, postponing the state of happiness forever. A child in school thinks he will be happy when he goes to college. Once in college, he thinks he will be happy when he starts earning. Then, he thinks he will be happy once he is married. The story goes on and on and that special day never arrives! All of one's life is spent in preparing to be happy someday in the future. It is like making the bed all night but having no time to sleep!

However, having no desires seems to be unrealistic and a rather gloomy state of affairs. Desires are spontaneous and innate. What to do then? This is the dilemma facing mankind.

There are two ways of looking at life. One is thinking: 'I will be happy after achieving a certain objective.' The second is believing: 'I am happy come what may!' Which one of these ways do you want to follow? If you look at your own life, you will find that life is 80 per cent joy and 20 per cent misery. But we hold on to the 20 per cent misery and make it 200 per cent!

The hand of happiness has not left anyone untouched. The wise one finds happiness in tiny things. For the wise, every act in life is an expression of happiness. For others, it is an expectation of joy. Everything you do can be done as an expression of happiness or your action can be that of expecting joy. The former spreads happiness in their environment, the latter struggles to achieve it. Negativity cannot remain without a support. Positivity – happiness – can be without any reason.

How many minutes, hours and days have you spent being happy from within? Those are the only moments you have really lived life. Those were perhaps the days when you were a small kid, completely blissful and happy when you were playing or doing something without a care in the world! You were living in the present and enjoying it. Living in the moment with joy, alertness, awareness and compassion is happiness.

Your senses are trying their best to find happiness for you all the time. But the senses have their limitations. How much music can the ears enjoy? How much food can you eat even if it is very tasty? The senses get tired too. You can feel sad without a reason. But you don't need a reason to be happy. When one is happy, the focus is on what one has and not what one lacks. There is satisfaction and contentment. That contentment brings dynamism. Some think that contentment will bring lethargy; on the contrary, frustration or discontentment has not brought about great creativity. One should not mistake contentment for laziness. If one is lazy, it is because of lack of energy/prana and low initiative. Prana is present in everything. In fact, we are floating in an ocean of prana. In the yogic terminology, happiness is a state of high prana, where dynamism is inherent.

Often, people who are unhappy cannot tolerate those who are happy. What comes out of the former is criticism, which is neither perceptually correct nor conceptually right. In a happy state, one would rather provide constructive criticism, daring the consequences. Every time you are unhappy or miserable, you are just realizing your own limitations and boundaries. It is limitations and boundaries that are the real causes of your disturbance. At that moment, what can you do? You can just be grateful and pray for peace and you will see that at that very moment you will start smiling again. And however hopeless the situation is, you will walk through it. A wise one is happy even in difficult times and the foolish one is unhappy even in good times.

In the ancient scriptures and Upanishads, the sages have quantified bliss. The joy you get from sensory pleasure is far lower than the emotional bliss one experiences from deep love, which is Samadhi. If conjugal happiness is considered to be 1 unit, the happiness of Samadhi is equivalent to 1000 units.

When you are happy, the mind expands and when you are unhappy the mind shrinks. So, whenever you think only 'mine, mine, mine', the mind is shrinking. Whenever the mind shrinks, it is bound to bring unhappiness. And when the mind expands it brings joy.

There is one kind of pleasure in acquiring and having and another in sharing and giving, which is the mature form of happiness. Happiness is when you want nothing, and you want to give; it is when the wanting and desires end and the sharing begins. A child loves to possess things and a grandmother finds happiness in sharing and giving. She will enjoy baking a cake and cooking a four-course meal when all her family members, including the grandchildren, are at home and her joy comes from cooking and serving. Though happiness begins during infancy, sometime in life it should mature to become the joy of giving – giving without expectation or any form of return.

One experiences happiness in change. What happens in change is that you move on from holding on to one object/person or place to another. However, you forget to note that though happiness is in the process of change, you tend to attribute it to the object you acquire. This brings happiness that can be temporary as you are focused only on the object rather than the change itself. The gap or space of leaving one object and changing to another has brought the happiness. Meditation can plug that gap.

We all have five (protective) sheaths to our existence called *panchakosha*. The first is the environment, the second the body, the third the mind, the forth emotions and the fifth bliss.

It is when you get in touch with the fifth sheath you get in touch with happiness. Whenever there is change, you unconsciously tap into this fifth sheath. This sheath, which is hidden deep within us, can be discovered with experience and practice. As the Vedas and the Upanishads proclaim: 'You are born of bliss and so is this world.'

When you are in touch with your inner being, then, irrespective of your outer state, you remain in a perpetual state of bliss. That is the goal of human endeavours. Often, we think this is too difficult to achieve, but, in fact, every baby is born this way. When basic needs are satiated, a child remains in a state of happiness. If you often ask a happy child 'what do you want?' the spontaneous answer would be 'nothing'. A yogi is a child and the purpose of yoga is to take us back to a state of innocence, by breaking down all barriers and bringing naturalness. There is a space within us that will remain ever pure, totally joyful and blissful, a space that can never be taken away from us.

The prerequisite to happiness is freedom and whenever one experiences freedom or a sense of expansion, happiness follows. The fluctuation of expansion and contraction, which happens in our consciousness with pleasant or unpleasant stimuli, causes one to experience sadness or happiness. If you can de-programme our consciousness from this reactive tendency to external stimuli, you can be unconditionally happy. It is natural to want happiness but happiness does not come alone. It brings along its twin sorrow. No one likes sorrow. In fact, everyone wants freedom from sorrow. This is also natural. When one realizes that along with happiness, there is also sorrow, the desire for freedom becomes stronger. When you stop craving for happiness you get freedom.

This is what moksha or liberation is: freedom from external stimuli. The practice of yoga and meditation gradually leads one to this state. In rare cases, this can be a sudden phenomenon. In fact, you can't do anything to bring happiness; you only have to remove the cause for sorrow. This is what the Great Sage Patanjali stated: 'Avoid the sorrow that has not come yet.' According to him, this is the purpose of yoga.

Wake up! Arise and enjoy all the flavours that the universe has provided to you.

wayne w. dyer

BEING HAPPY

Unclutter your life. Clear your calendar of unwanted activities. Be sure to keep your free time free. Take time for meditation and yoga. Return to simplicity of nature. Put distance between yourself and your critics. Slow Down. Eschew Debt.

HAVING BEEN IN THE BUSINESS OF HUMAN development for most of my life, the question I most frequently hear is: 'How do I go about getting what I want?' My response is: 'If you become what you think about, and what you think about is getting what you want, then you'll stay in a state of wanting. So, the answer to how to get what you want is to reframe the question to: How do I go about getting what I intend to create?' My answer is: 'You get what you intend to create by being in harmony with the power of intention, which is responsible for all of creation.' Become just like intention and you'll co-create all that you contemplate. When you become one with intention, you're transcending the ego-mind and becoming the universal all-creative mind. John Randolph Price writes in *A Spiritual Philosophy for the New World*: 'Until you transcend the ego, you can do nothing but add to the insanity of the world. That statement should delight you rather than create despair, for it removes the burden from your shoulders.'

Begin to remove that ego burden from your shoulders and reconnect to intention. When you lay your ego aside and return to that from which you originally emanated, you'll begin to immediately see the power of intention working with, for, and through you in a multitude of ways. Here are those seven faces revisited to help you to begin to make them a part of your life.

1. Be creative

Being creative means trusting your own purpose and having an attitude of unbending intent in your daily thoughts and activities. Staying creative means giving form to your personal intentions. A way to start giving them form is to literally put them in writing. To express your creativity and put your own intentions into the world of the manifest, I recommend that you practice Japa, a technique first offered by the ancient Vedas. Japa meditation is the repetition of the sound of the names of God while simultaneously focusing on what you intend to manifest. Repeating the sound within the name of God while asking for what you want generates creative energy to manifest your desires. And your desires are the movement of the universal mind within you. Now, you may be skeptical about the feasibility of such an undertaking. Well, I ask you to open yourself to this idea of Japa as an expression of your creative link to intention. I consider meditating and practicing Japa essential in the quest to realign yourself with the power of intention. That power is Creation, and you need to be in your own unique state of creativity to collaborate with the power of intention. Meditation and Japa are surefire ways to do so.

2. Be Kind

A fundamental attribute of the supreme originating power is kindness. All that's manifested is brought here to thrive. It takes a kindly power to want what it creates to thrive and multiply. Were this not the case, then all that's created would be destroyed by the same power that created it. Make an effort to live in cheerful kindness. It's a much higher energy than sadness or malevolence, and it makes the manifestation of your desires possible. *Its through giving that we receive*; it's through acts of kindness directed toward others that our immune systems are strengthened and even our serotonin levels increased!

Low energy thoughts that weaken us fall in the realm of shame, anger, hatred, judgement, and fear. Each of these inner thoughts weakens us and inhibits us from attracting into our lives what we desire. If we become what we think about, and what we think about is what's wrong with the world and how angry and ashamed and fearful we are, it stands to reason that we'll act on those unkind thoughts and become what we're thinking about. When you think, feel, and act kindly, you give yourself the opportunity to be like the power of intention. When you're thinking and acting otherwise, you've left the field of intention, and you've assured yourself of feeling cheated by the all-creative Spirit of intent.

— *Kindness toward yourself.* Think of yourself like this: There's a universal intelligence subsisting throughout nature inherent in every one of its manifestations. You are one of those manifestations. You are a piece of this universal intelligence – a slice of God, if you will. Be good to God, since all that God created was good. Be good to yourself. You are God manifested, and that's reason enough to treat yourself kindly. Remind yourself that you want to be kind to yourself in all the choices that you make about your daily life. Treat yourself with kindness when you eat, exercise, play, work, love, and everything else. Treating yourself kindly will hasten your ability to connect to intention.

— *Kindness toward others.* A basic tenet of getting along and being happy, as well as enlisting the assistance of others toward achieving all that you want to attract, is that people want to help you and do things for you. When you're kind to others, you receive kindness in return. A boss who's unkind gets very little cooperation from his employees. Being unkind with children makes them want to get even rather than help you out. Kindness given is kindness returned. If you wish to connect to intention and become someone who achieves all of your objectives in life, you're going to need the assistance of a multitude of folks. By practicing extending kindness everywhere, you'll find support showing up in ways that you could never have predicted.

This idea of extending kindness is particularly relevant in how you deal with people who are helpless, elderly, mentally challenged, poor, disabled, and so on. These people are all part of God's perfection. They, too, have a divine purpose, and since all of us are connected to each other through Spirit, their purpose and intent is also connected to you. Here's a brief story that will touch you at the heart level. It suggests that those whom we meet who are less than able to care for themselves may have come here to teach us something about the perfection of intention. Read it and know that this kind of thinking, feeling, and behavior empowers you to connect to intention through matching its kindness with your own.

In Brooklyn, New York, Chush is a school that caters to learning-disabled children. Some children remain in Chush for their entire school career, while others can be main-streamed into conventional schools. At a Chush fundraiser dinner, the father of a Chush child delivered a speech that would never be forgotten by all who attended. After extolling the school and its dedicated staff, he cried out: 'Where is the perfection in my son, Shaya? Everything God does is done with perfection.

But my child cannot understand things as other children do. My child cannot remember facts and figures as other children do. Where is God's perfection?' The audience was shocked by the question, pained by the father's anguish, and stilled by the piercing query.

'I believe,' the father answered, 'that when God brings a child like this into the world, the perfection that he seeks is in the way people react to this child.' He then told the following story about his son, Shaya:

One afternoon Shaya and his father walked past a park where some boys Shaya knew were playing baseball. Shaya asked: 'Do you think they'll let me play?' Shaya's father knew that his son was not at all athletic and that most boys would not want him on their team. But Shaya's father understood that if his son was chosen to play, it would give him a sense of belonging. Shaya's father approached one of the boys on the field and asked if Shaya could play. The boy looked around for guidance from his teammates. Getting none, he took matters into his own hands and said: 'We're losing by six runs, and the game is in the eighth inning. I guess he can be on our team, and we'll try to put him up to bat in the ninth inning.' Shaya's father was ecstatic as Shaya smiled broadly. Shaya was told to put on a glove and go out to play in center field. In the bottom of the eighth inning, Shaya's team scored a few runs but was still behind by three. In the bottom of the ninth inning, Shaya's team scored again, and now had two outs and the bases loaded, with the potential winning run on base, Shaya was scheduled to be up. Would the team actually let Shaya bat at this juncture and give away their chance to win the game?

Surprisingly, Shaya was given the bat. Everyone knew that it was all but impossible because Shaya didn't even know how to hold the bat properly, let alone hit with it. However, as Shaya stepped up to the plate, the pitcher moved a few steps to lob the ball in softly so Shaya could at least be able to make contact. The first pitch came in, and Shaya swung clumsily and missed. One of Shaya's teammates came up to Shaya, and together they held the bat and faced the pitcher waiting for the next pitch. The pitcher again took a few steps forward to toss the ball softly toward Shaya. As the pitch came in, Shaya and his teammate swung the bat, and together they hit a slow ground ball to the pitcher. The pitcher picked up the soft grounder and could easily have thrown the ball to the first baseman. Shaya would have been out and that would have ended the game. Instead, the pitcher took the ball and threw it on a high arc to right field far beyond the reach of the first baseman. Everyone started yelling: 'Shaya, run to first. Run to first.' Never in his life had Shaya run to first. He scampered down the baseline wide-eyed and startled. By the time he reached first base, the right-fielder had the ball. He could have thrown the ball to the second baseman who would tag out Shaya, who was still running. But the right-fielder understood what the pitcher's intentions were, so he threw the ball high and far over the third baseman's head. Everyone yelled: 'Run to second, run to second.' Shaya ran toward second base as the runners ahead of him deliriously circled the bases toward home. As Shaya reached second base, the opposing shortstop ran to him, turned him in the direction of third base, and shouted: 'Run to third.' As Shaya rounded third, the boys from both teams ran behind him screaming: 'Shaya, run home.' Shaya ran home, stepped on home plate, and all 18 boys lifted him on their shoulders and made him the hero, as he had just hit a 'grand slam' and won the game for his team.

'That day,' said the father softly with tears now rolling down his face, 'those 18 boys reached their level of God's perfection.'

If you don't feel a tug in your heart and a tear in your eye after reading this story, then it's unlikely that you'll ever know the magic of connecting back to the kindness of the supreme all-originating Source.

— *Kindness toward all of life*. In the ancient teachings of Patanjali, we're reminded that all living creatures are impacted dramatically by those who remain steadfast in the absence of thoughts of harm directed outward.

Practice kindness toward all animals, tiny and huge, the entire kingdom of life on Earth such as the forests, the deserts, the beaches, and all that has the essence of life pulsating within it. You can't reconnect to your Source and know the power of intention in your life without the assistance of the environment. You're connected to this environment. Without gravity, you can't walk. Without the water, you can't live a day. Without the forests, the sky, the atmosphere, the vegetation, the minerals – all of it – your desire to manifest and reach intention is meaningless.

Extend thoughts of kindness everywhere. Practice kindness toward Earth by picking up a piece of litter that's on your path, or saying a silent prayer of gratitude for the existence of rain, the color of flowers, or even the paper you hold in your hand that was donated by a tree. The universe responds in kind to what you elect to radiate outward. If you say with kindness in your voice and in your heart: 'How may I serve you?' the universe's response will be: 'How may I serve you as well?' It's attractor energy. It's this spirit of cooperation with all of life that emerges from the essence of intention. And this spirit of kindness is one that you must learn to match if connecting back to intention is your desire.

3. Be Love

Ponder these words thoughtfully: God is love, 'and he that dwelleth in love dwelleth in me, and I in him.'

That is God talking, so to speak. You were intended out of love, you must be love in order to intend. Volumes have been written about love, and still we have as many definitions for this word as we have people to offer them. For the purposes of this essay, I'd like you to think about love in the following two ways.

— *Love is cooperation rather than competition.* What I'd like you to be able to experience right here in physical form on planet Earth is the essence of the spiritual plane. If this were possible, it would mean that your very life is a manifestation of love. Were this to be true for you, you'd see all of life living together in harmony and cooperating with each other. You'd sense that the power of intention that originates all life cooperates with all other life forms to ensure growth and survival. You'd note that we all share the same life force, and the same invisible intelligence that beats my heart and your heart, beats the heart of everyone on the planet.

— *Love is the force behind the will of God.* I'm not suggesting the kind of love that we define as affection or sentiment. Nor is this kind of love a feeling that seeks to please and press favors on others. Imagine a kind of love that is the power of intention, the very energy that is the cause behind all of creation. It's the spiritual vibration that carries divine intentions from formless to concrete expression. It creates new form, changes matter, vivifies all things, and holds the cosmos together beyond time and space. It's in every one of us. It is what God is.

I recommend that you pour your love into your immediate environment and hold to this practice on an hourly basis if possible. Remove all unloving thoughts from your mind, and practice kindness in all of your thoughts, words, and actions. Cultivate this love in your immediate circle of acquaintances and family, and ultimately it will expand to your community and globally as well. Extend this love deliberately to those you feel have harmed you in any way or caused you to experience suffering. The more you can extend this love, the closer you come to being loved and it's in the beingness of love that intention is reached and manifestation flourishes.

4. Be Beauty

Emily Dickinson wrote: 'Beauty is not caused. It is...' As you awaken to your divine nature, you'll begin to appreciate beauty in everything you see, touch, and experience. Beauty and truth are synonymous as you read in John Keats's famous observation in *Ode on a Grecian Urn*: 'Beauty is truth, truth beauty.' This means, of course, that the creative Spirit brings things into the world of boundaries to thrive and flourish and expand. And it wouldn't do so were it not infatuated with the beauty of every manifested creature, including you. Thus, to come back into conscious contact with your Source so as to regain the power of your Source is to look for and experience beauty in all of your undertakings. Life, truth, beauty. These are all symbols for the same thing, an aspect of the God-force.

When you lose this awareness, you lose the possibility of connecting to intention. You were brought into this world from that which perceived you as an expression of beauty. It couldn't have done so if it thought you to be otherwise, for if it has the power to create; it also possesses the power not to do so. The choice to do so is predicated on the supposition that you're an expression of loving beauty. This is true for everything and everyone that emanates from the power of intention.

Here's a favorite story of mine that illustrates appreciating beauty where once you didn't. It was told by Swami Chidvilasananda, better known as Gurumayi, in her beautiful book, *Kindle My Heart*.

There was a man who did not like his in-laws because he felt they took up more space in the house than they should. He went to a teacher who lived nearby, as he had heard a lot about him, and he said, 'Please do something! I cannot bear my in-laws anymore. I love my wife, but my inlaws – never! They take up so much space in the house; somehow I feel they are always in my way.'

The teacher asked him, 'Do you have some chickens?'

'Yes, I do,' he said.

'Then put all your chickens inside the house.'

He did what the teacher said and then went back to him.

The teacher asked, 'Problem solved?'

He said, 'No! It's worse.'

Do you have any sheep?'

'Yes.'

Bring all the sheep inside.'He did so and returned to the teacher. 'Problem solved?'

'No! It's getting worse'

Do you have a dog?'

'Yes, I have several.'

'Take all those dogs into the house.'

Finally, the man ran back to the teacher and said, I came to you for help, but you are making my life worse than ever!'

The teacher said to him, 'Now send all the chickens, sheep, and dogs back outside.'

The man went home and emptied the house of all the animals. There was so much space! He went back to the teacher. 'Thank you! Thank you!' he said. *'You have solved all my problems.'*

5. Be Ever-Expansive

The next time you see a garden full of flowers, observe the flowers that are alive, and compare them to the flowers that you believe are dead. What's the difference? The dried-up, *dead* flowers are no longer growing, while the alive flowers are indeed still growing. The all-emerging universal force that intended you into beingness and commences all life is always growing, and perpetually expanding. As with all seven of these faces of intention, by reason of its universality, it must have a common nature with yours. By being in an ever-expanding state and growing intellectually, emotionally, and spiritually, you're identifying with the universal mind.

By staying in a state of readiness in which you're not attached to what you used to think or be, and by thinking from the end and staying open to receiving divine guidance, you abide by the law of growth and are receptive to the power of intention.

6. Be Abundant

Intention is endlessly abundant. There's no scarcity in the universal invisible world of Spirit. The cosmos itself is without end. How could there be an end to the universe? What would be at the end? A wall? So how thick is the wall? And what's on the other side of it? As you contemplate connecting to intention, know in your heart that any attitude you have that reflects a scarcity consciousness will hold you back. A reminder here is in order. You must match intention's attributes with your own in order to capitalize on those powers in your life.

Abundance is what God's kingdom is about. Imagine God thinking, *I can't produce any more oxygen today, I'm just too tired; this universe is big enough already, I think I'll erect that wall and bring this expansion thing to a halt.*

Impossible! You emerged from a consciousness that was and is unlimited. So what's to prevent you from rejoining that limitless awareness in your mind and holding on to these pictures regardless of what goes before you? What prevents you is the conditioning you've been exposed to during your life, which you can change today – in the next few minutes if you so desire.

When you shift to an abundance mind-set, you repeat to yourself over and over again that you're unlimited because you emanated from the inexhaustible supply of intention. As this picture solidifies, you begin to act on this attitude of unbending intent. There's no other possibility. We become what we think about, and as Emerson reminded us: 'The ancestor to every action is a thought.' As these thoughts of plentitude and excessive sufficiency become your way of thinking, the all-creating force to which you're always connected will begin to work with you, in harmony with your thoughts, just as it worked with you in harmony with your thoughts of scarcity. If you think you can't manifest abundance into your life, you'll see intention agreeing with you, and assisting you in the fulfillment of meager expectations!

***

I seem to have arrived into this world fully connected to the abundance attributes of the spiritual world from which I emanated. As a child growing up in foster homes, with poverty consciousness all around me, I was the "richest" kid in the orphanage, so to speak. I always thought I could have money jingling in my pocket. I pictured it there, and I consequently acted on that picture. I'd collect soda-pop bottles, shovel snow, bag groceries, cut lawns, carry out people's ashes from their coal furnaces, clean up yards, paint fences, baby-sit, deliver newspapers, and on and on. And always, the universal force of abundance worked *with* me in providing opportunities. A snowstorm was a giant blessing for me. So too were discarded bottles by the side of the road, and little old ladies who needed help carrying their groceries to their automobiles.

Today, over a half century later, I still have that abundance mentality. I've never been without several jobs at one time throughout many economic slumps over my lifetime. I made large amounts of money as a schoolteacher by starting a driver-education business after school hours. I began a lecture series in Port Washington, New York, on Monday evenings for 30 or so local residents to supplement my income as a professor at St. John's University, and that Monday-night series became an audience of over a thousand people in the high school auditorium. Each lecture was tape-recorded by a staff member, and those tapes led to the outline for my first book to the public, which was called *Your Erroneous Zones*.

One of the attendees was the wife of a literary agent in New York City who encouraged him to contact me about writing a book. That man, Arthur Pine, became like a father to me and helped me meet key publishing people in New York. And the same story of unlimited thinking goes on and on. I saw the book *from the end* becoming a tool for everyone in the country and proceeded to go to every large city in America to tell people about it.

The universal Spirit has always worked with me in bringing my thoughts of unlimited abundance into my life. The right people would magically appear. The right break would come along. The help I needed would seemingly manifest out of nowhere. And in a sense, I'm still collecting pop bottles, shoveling snow, and carrying out groceries for little old ladies today. My vision hasn't changed, although the playing field is enlarged. It's all about having an inner picture of abundance, thinking in unlimited ways, being open to the guidance that intention provides when you're in a state of rapport with it – and then being in a state of ecstatic gratitude and awe for how this whole thing works. Every time I see a coin on the street, I stop, pick it up, put it into my pocket, and say out loud: 'Thank you, God, for this symbol of abundance that keeps flowing into my life.' Never once have I asked: 'Why only a penny, God? You know I need a lot more than that.'

Today, I arise at 4 A.M. with a knowing that my writing will complete what I've already envisioned in the contemplations of my imagination. The writing flows, and letters arrive from intention's manifest abundance urging me to read a particular book, or to talk to a unique individual, and I know that it's all working in perfect, abundant unity. The phone rings, and just what I need to hear is resonating in my ear. I get up to get a glass of water, and my eyes fall on a book that's been on my shelf for 20 years, but this time I'm compelled to pick it up. I open it, and I'm once again being directed by spirit's willingness to assist and guide me as long as I stay in harmony with it. It goes on and on, and I'm reminded of Jelaluddin Rumi's poetic words from 800 years ago: 'Sell your cleverness, and purchase bewilderment.'

7. Be Receptive

The universal mind is ready to respond to anyone who recognizes their true relationship to it. It will reproduce whatever conception of itself you impress upon it. In other words, it's receptive to all who remain in harmony with it and stay in a relationship of reverence for it. The issue becomes a question of your receptivity to the power of intention. Stay connected and know you'll receive all that this power is capable of offering. Take it on by yourself as separate from the universal mind (an impossibility, but nevertheless, a strong belief of the ego), and you remain eternally disconnected.

The nature of the universal mind is peaceful. It isn't receptive to force or violence. It works in its own time and rhythm, allowing everything to emanate by and by. It's in no hurry because it's outside of time. It's always in the eternal now. Try getting down on your hands and knees and hurrying along a tiny tomato plant sprout.

Universal Spirit is at work peacefully, and your attempts to rush it or tug new life into full creative flower will destroy the entire process. Being receptive means allowing your 'senior partner' to handle your life for you. *I accept the guidance and assistance of the same force that created me, I let go of my ego, and I trust in this wisdom to move at its own peaceful pace. I make no demands on it.* This is how the all-creating field of intention creates. This is how you must think in order to reconnect to your Source. You practice meditation because it allows you to receive the inner knowing of making conscious contact with God. By being peaceful, quiet, and receptive, you pattern yourself in the image of God, and you regain the power of your Source.

***

If you practice raising your energy level by being cognizant of your immediate environment, you'll move rather rapidly toward intention and remove all of those self-imposed roadblocks. The obstacles are in the low-energy spectrum.

A Mini-Programme for Raising Your Energy Vibrations:

Here's a short list of suggestions for moving your energy field to a higher, faster vibration. This will help you accomplish the twofold objective of removing the barriers and allowing the power of intention to work with and through you.

Become conscious of your thoughts. Every thought you have impacts you. By shifting in the middle of a weakening thought to one that strengthens, you raise your energy vibration and strengthen yourself and the immediate energy field. For example, in the midst of saying something to one of my teenage children that was intended to make her feel ashamed of her conduct, I stopped and reminded myself that there's no remedy in condemnation. I proceeded to extend love and understanding by asking her how she felt about her self-defeating behavior and what she'd like to do to correct it. The shift raised the energy level and led to a productive conversation.

Raising the energy level to a place where my daughter and I connected to the power of intention took place in a split second of my becoming aware of my low-energy thinking and making a decision to raise it. We all have the ability to call this presence and power of intention into action when we become conscious of our thoughts.

Make meditation a regular practice in your life. Even if it's only for a few moments each day while sitting at a stoplight, this practice is vital. Take some time to be silent, and repeat the sound of God as an inner mantra. Meditation allows you to make conscious contact with your Source and regain the power of intention by assisting you in cultivating a receptivity that matches up with the force of creation.

Become conscious of the foods you eat. There are foods that calibrate low, and there are high-energy foods as well. Foods with toxic chemicals sprayed on them will make you weak even if you have no idea that the toxins are present. Artificial foods such as sweeteners are low-energy products. In general, foods high in alkalinity such as fruits, vegetables, nuts, soy, non-yeast breads, and virgin olive oil calibrate at the high end and will strengthen you on muscle testing, while highly acidic foods such as flour-based cereals, meats, dairy, and sugars calibrate at the lower energies, which will weaken you. This is not an absolute for everyone; however, you can detect how you feel after consuming certain foods, and if you feel weak, lethargic, and fatigued, you can be pretty sure you've allowed yourself to become a low-energy system, which will attract more of the same low energy into your life.

Retreat from low-energy substances. Alcohol, and virtually all artificial drugs, legal and otherwise, lower your body's energy level and weaken you. Furthermore, they put you in a position to continue to attract more disempowering energy into your life. Simply by consuming low-energy substances, you'll find people with similar low energy showing up regularly in your life. They'll want to buy those substances for you, party with you as you get high, and urge you to do it again after your body recovers from the devastation of these low-energy substances.

Become conscious of the energy level of the music you listen to. Harsh, pounding, musical vibrations with repetitive, loud sounds lower your energy level and weaken you and your ability to make conscious contact with intention. Similarly, the lyrics of hate, pain, anguish, fear, and violence are low energies sending weakening messages to your subconscious and infiltrating your life with similar attractor energies. If you want to attract violence, then listen to the lyrics of violence and make violent music a part of your life. If you want to attract peace and love, then listen to the higher musical vibrations and lyrics that reflect your desires.

Become aware of the energy levels of your home environment. Prayers, paintings, crystals, statues, spiritual passages, books, magazines, the colors on your walls, and even the arrangement of your furniture all create energy into which you're catapulted for at least half of your waking life. While this may seem silly or absurd, I urge you to transcend your conditioned thinking and have a mind that's open to everything. The ancient Chinese art of feng shui has been with us for thousands of years and is a gift from our ancestors. It describes ways to increase the energy field of our home and workplace. Become aware of how being in high-energy surroundings impacts us in ways that strengthen our lives and remove barriers to our connection to intention.

Reduce your exposure to the very low energy of commercial and cable television. Children in America see 12,000 simulated murders in their living room before their 14th birthday! Television news programming puts a heavy emphasis on bringing the bad and the ugly into your home, and in large part, leaving out the good. It's a constant stream of negativity that invades your living space and attracts more of the same into your life. Violence is the main ingredient of television entertainment, interspersed with commercial breaks sponsored by the huge drug cartels telling us that happiness is found in their pills! The viewing public is told that it needs all sorts of low-energy medicines to overcome every mental and physical malady known to humankind.

My conclusion is that the majority of television shows provide a steady stream of low energy most of the time..

Enhance your energy field with photographs. You may find it difficult to believe that photography is a form of energy reproduction and that every photograph contains energy. See for yourself by strategically placing photographs taken in moments of happiness, love, and receptivity to spiritual help around your living quarters, in your workplace, in your automobile, and even on your clothing or in a pocket or wallet. Arrange photographs of nature, animals, and expressions of joy and love in your environment, and let their energy radiate into your heart and provide you with their higher frequency.

Become conscious of the energy levels of your acquaintances, friends, and extended family. You can raise your own energy levels by being in the energy field of others who resonate closely to spiritual consciousness. Choose to be in close proximity to people who are empowering, who appeal to your sense of connection to intention, who see the greatness in you, who feel connected to God, and who live a life that gives evidence that Spirit has found celebration through them. Recall that higher energy nullifies and converts lower energy, so be conscious of being in the presence of, and interacting with, higher-energy people who are connected to Spirit and living the life they were intended to. Stay in the energy field of higher-energy people and your anger, hate, fear, and depression will melt – magically converting to the higher expressions of intention.

Monitor your activities and where they take place. Avoid low-energy fields where there's excessive alcohol, drug consumption, or violent behavior, and gatherings where religious or ethnic exclusion and vitriolic prejudice or judgement are the focus. All of these kinds of venues discourage you from raising your energy and encourage you to match up with lower, debilitating energy. Immerse yourself in nature, appreciating its beauty, spending time camping, hiking, swimming, taking nature walks, and reveling in the natural world. Attend lectures on spirituality, take a yoga class, give or receive a massage, visit monasteries or meditation centers, and commit to helping others in need with visits to the elderly in geriatric centers or sick children in hospitals. Every activity has an energy field. Choose to be in places where the energy fields reflect the seven faces of intention.

Extend acts of kindness, asking for nothing in return. Anonymously extend financial aid to those less fortunate, and do it from the kindness of your heart, expecting not even a thank you.

Activate your magnificent obsession by learning to be kind while keeping your ego – which expects to be told how wonderful you are – out of the picture completely. This is an essential activity for connecting to intention because the universal all-creating Spirit returns acts of kindness with the response: *How may I be kind to you?*

Pick up some litter and place it in a proper receptacle and tell no one about your actions. In fact, spend several hours doing nothing but cleaning and clearing out messes that you didn't create. Any act of kindness extended toward yourself, others, or your environment matches you up with the kindness inherent in the universal power of intention. It's an energizer for you, and causes this kind of energy to flow back into your life.

This poignant story 'The Valentine,' by Ruth McDonald, illustrates the kind of giving I'm suggesting here. The little boy symbolizes the magnificent obsession I just referred to.

He was a shy little boy, not very popular with the other children in Grade One. As Valentine's Day approached, his mother was delighted when he asked her one evening to sit down and write the names of all the children in his class so that he could make a Valentine for each. Slowly he remembered each name aloud, and his mother recorded them on a piece of paper. He worried endlessly for fear he would forget someone.

Armed with a book of Valentines to cut out, with scissors and crayons and paste, he plodded his conscientious way down the list. When each one was finished, his mother printed the name on a piece of paper and watched him laboriously copy it. As the pile of finished Valentines grew, so did his satisfaction.

About this time, his mother began to worry whether the other children would make Valentines for him. He hurried home so fast each afternoon to get on with his task, that it seemed likely the other children playing along the street would forget his existence altogether. How absolutely horrible if he went off to the party armed with 37 tokens of love – and no one had remembered him! She wondered if there were some way she could sneak a few Valentines among those he was making so that he would be sure of receiving at least a few. But he watched his hoard so jealously, and counted them over so lovingly, that there was no chance to slip in an extra. She assumed a mother's most normal role, that of patient waiting.

The day of the Valentine box finally arrived, and she watched him trudge off down the snowy street, a box of heart-shaped cookies in one hand, a shopping-bag clutched in the other with 37 neat tokens of his labor. She watched him with a burning heart. 'Please, God,' she prayed, 'let him get at least a few!'

All afternoon her hands were busy here and there, but her heart was at the school. At half-past three she took her knitting and sat with studied coincidence in a chair that gave a full view of the street.

Finally, he appeared, alone. Her heart sank. Up the street he came, turning every once in a while to back up a few steps into the wind. She strained her eyes to see his face. At that distance it was just a rosy blur.

It was not until he turned in at the walk that she saw it – the one lone Valentine clutched in his little red mitt. Only one. After all his work. And from the teacher probably. The knitting blurred before her eyes. If only you could stand between your child and life! She laid down her work and walked to meet him at the door.

'What rosy cheeks!' she said. 'Here, let me untie your scarf. Were the cookies good?'

He turned toward her a face shining with happiness and complete fulfillment. 'Do you know what?' he said. 'I didn't forget a one. Not a single one!'

Be specific when you affirm your intentions to raise your energy level and create your desires. Place your affirmations in strategic places where you'll notice and read them throughout the day. For example: I intend to attract the job I desire into my life. I intend to be able to afford the specific automobile I envision myself driving by the 30th of next month. I intend to donate two hours of my time this week to the underprivileged. I intend to heal myself of this persistent fatigue.

Written affirmations have an energy of their own and will guide you in raising your energy level. I practice this myself. A woman named Lynn Hall who lives in Toronto sent me a beautiful plaque that I look at each day. In her letter she stated: 'Here is a gift for you, written solely for you in an effort to convey heartfelt gratitude for the blessing of your presence in my life. That said, I am sure that the sentiment is a universal one speaking for every other soul on the planet who has experienced the same good fortune. May the light and love that you emit forever reflect back to you in joyful abundance, Dr. Dyer.' The beautiful etched-in-soul plaque reads like this:

Spirit
Has found
Great voice
In you.
In vibrant truths,
And joyful splendor.

Spirit
Has found
Revelation
Through you,
In resonant
And reflective ways.
Spirit
Has found
Celebration
Through you,
In infinite expanses
And endless reach.
To
All those
Awakened
To the
Grace of
Your gifts –
Spirit
Has found
Both
Wings
And
Light.

I read these words daily to remind me of my connection to Spirit, and allow the words to flow from my heart to yours, fulfilling my intentions and hopefully helping you do the same.

As frequently as possible, hold thoughts of forgiveness in your mind. In muscle testing, when you hold a thought of revenge, you'll go weak, while a thought of forgiveness keeps you strong. Revenge, anger, and hatred are exceedingly low energies that keep you from matching up with the attributes of the universal force. A simple thought of forgiveness toward anyone who may have angered you in the past – without any action taken on your part – will raise you to the level of Spirit and aid you in your individual intentions.

You can either serve Spirit with your mind or use that same mind to divorce yourself from Spirit. Married to the seven faces of spiritual intention, you connect to that power. Divorced, your self-importance, your ego, takes over.

***

Your Self-Importance

In *The Fire from Within*, Carlos Castaneda hears these words from his sorcerer teacher: 'Self-importance is man's greatest enemy. What weakens him is feeling offended by the deeds and misdeeds of his fellow man. Self-importance requires that one spend most of one's life offended by something or someone.' This is a major impediment to connecting to intention; you can all too easily create a no match here.

Basically, your feelings of self-importance are what make you feel special, so let's deal with this concept of being special. It's essential that you have a strong self-concept and that you feel unique. The problem is when you misidentify who you truly are by identifying yourself as your body, your achievements, and your possessions. Then you identify people who have accomplished less as inferior, and your self-important superiority causes you to be constantly offended in one way or another. This misidentification is the source of most of your problems, as well as most of the problems of humankind. Feeling *special* leads us to our self-importance. Castaneda writes later in his life, many years after his initial emergence into the world of sorcery, about the futility of self-importance: 'The more I thought about it, and the more I talked to and observed myself and my fellow men, the more intense the conviction that something was rendering us incapable of any activity or any interaction or any thought that didn't have the self as its focal point.'

With the self as a focal point, you sustain the illusion that you are your body, which is a completely separate entity from all others. This sense of separateness leads you to compete rather than cooperate with everyone else. Ultimately, it's a no match with Spirit, and becomes a huge obstacle to your connection to the power of intention. In order to relinquish your self-importance, you'll have to become aware of how entrenched it is in your life. Ego is simply an *idea of who you are* that you carry around with you. As such, it can't be surgically removed by having an egoectomy! This *idea of who you* think you are will persistently erode any possibility you have of connecting to intention.

Seven Steps for Overcoming Ego's Hold on You

Here are seven suggestions to help you transcend ingrained ideas of self-importance. All of these are designed to help prevent you from falsely identifying with the self-important ego.

1. Stop being offended

The behavior of others isn't a reason to be immobilized. That which offends you only weakens you. If you're looking for occasions to be offended, you'll find them at every turn. This is your ego at work convincing you that the world shouldn't be the way it is. But you can become an appreciator of life and match up with the universal Spirit of Creation. You can't reach the power of intention by being offended. By all means, act to eradicate the horrors of the world, which emanate from massive ego identification, but stay in peace. As A Course in Miracles reminds us: Peace is of God, you who are part of God are not at home except in his peace. Being offended creates the same destructive energy that offended you in the first place and leads to attack, counterattack, and war.

2. Let go of your need to win.

Ego loves to divide us up into winners and losers. The pursuit of winning is a surefire means to avoid conscious contact with intention. Why? Because ultimately, winning is impossible all of the time. Someone out there will be faster, luckier, younger, stronger, and smarter— and back you'll go to feeling worthless and insignificant.

You're not your winnings or your victories. You may enjoy competing, and have fun in a world where winning is everything, but you don't have to be there in your thoughts. There are no losers in a world where we all share the same energy source. All you can say on a given day is that you performed at a certain level in comparison to the levels of others on that day. But today is another day, with other competitors and new circumstances to consider. You're still the infinite presence in a body that's another day (or decade) older. Let go of *needing* to win by not agreeing that the opposite of winning is losing. That's ego's fear. If your body isn't performing in a *winning* fashion on this day, it simply doesn't matter when you aren't identifying exclusively with your ego. Be the observer, noticing and enjoying it all without needing to win a trophy. Be at peace, and match up with the energy of intention. And ironically, although you'll hardly notice it, more of those victories will show up in your life as you pursue them less.

3. Let go of your need to be right

Ego is the source of a lot of conflict and dissension because it pushes you in the direction of making other people wrong. When you're hostile, you've disconnected from the power of intention. The creative Spirit is kind, loving, and receptive; and free of anger, resentment, or bitterness. Letting go of your need to be right in your discussions and relationships is like saying to ego, I'm not a slave to you. I want to embrace kindness, and I reject your need to be right. In fact, I'm going to offer this person a chance to feel better by saying that she's right, and thank her for pointing me in the direction of truth.

When you let go of the need to be right, you're able to strengthen your connection to the power of intention. But keep in mind that ego is a determined combatant. I've seen people willing to die rather than let go of being right. I've seen people end otherwise beautiful relationships by sticking to their need to be right. I urge you to let go of this ego-driven need to be right by stopping yourself in the middle of an argument and asking yourself, Do I want to be right or be happy? When you choose the happy, loving, spiritual mode, your connection to intention is strengthened. These moments ultimately expand your new connection to the power of intention. The universal Source will begin to collaborate with you in creating the life you were intended to live.

4. Let go of your need to be superior

True nobility isn't about being better than someone else. It's about being better than you used to be. Stay focused on your growth, with a constant awareness that no one on this planet is any better than anyone else. We all emanate from the same creative life force. We all have a mission to realize our intended essence; all that we need to fulfill our destiny is available to us. None of this is possible when you see yourself as superior to others. It's an old saw, but nonetheless true: *We are all equal in the eyes of God.* Let go of your need to feel superior by seeing the unfolding of God in everyone. Don't assess others on the basis of their appearance, achievements, possessions, and other indices of ego. When you project feelings of superiority, that's what you get back, leading to resentments and ultimately hostile feelings. These feelings become the vehicle that takes you farther away from intention.

5. *Let go of your need to have more*

The mantra of the ego is *more*. It's never satisfied. No matter how much you achieve or acquire, your ego will insist that it isn't enough. You'll find yourself in a perpetual state of striving, and eliminate the possibility of ever arriving. Yet in reality, you've already arrived, and how you choose to use this present moment of your life is your choice. Ironically, when you stop needing more, more of what you desire seems to arrive in your life. Since you're detached from the need for it, you find it easier to pass it along to others, because you realize how little you need in order to be satisfied and at peace.

The universal Source is content with itself, constantly

expanding and creating new life, never trying to hold on to its creations for its own selfish means. It creates and lets go. As you let go of ego's need to have more, you unify with that Source. You create, attract to yourself, and let it go, never demanding that more come your way. As an appreciator of all that shows up, you learn the powerful lesson St. Francis of Assisi taught: ' . . . it is in giving that we receive.' By allowing abundance to flow to and through you, you match up with your Source and guarantee that this energy will continue to flow.

6. Let go of identifying yourself on the basis of your achievements

This may be a difficult concept if you think you *are* your achievements. *God writes all the music, God sings all the songs, God builds all the buildings, God is the source of all your achievements.* I can hear your ego loudly protesting. Nevertheless, stay tuned to this idea. All emanates from Source! You and that Source are one! You're not this body and its accomplishments. You are the observer. Notice it all; and be grateful for the abilities you've been given, the motivation to achieve, and the stuff you've accumulated. But give all the credit to the power of intention, which brought you into existence and which you're a materialized part of. The less you need to take credit for your achievements and the more connected you stay to the seven faces of intention, the more you're free to achieve, and the more will show up for you. It's when you attach yourself to those achievements and believe that you alone are doing all of those things that you leave the peace and the gratitude of your Source.

7. Let go of your reputation

Your reputation is not located in you. It resides in the minds of others. Therefore, you have no control over it at all. If you speak to 30 people, you will have 30 reputations. Connecting to intention means listening to your heart and conducting yourself based on what your inner voice tells you is your purpose here. If you're overly concerned with how you're going to be perceived by everyone, then you've disconnected yourself from intention and allowed the opinions of others to guide you. This is your ego at work. It's an illusion that stands between you and the power of intention. There's nothing you can't do, unless you disconnect from the power source and become convinced that your purpose is to prove to others how masterful and superior you are and spend your energy attempting to win a giant reputation among other egos. Do what you do because your inner voice – always connected to and grateful to your Source – so directs you. Stay on purpose, detach from outcome, and take responsibility for what does reside in you: your character. Leave your reputation for others to debate; it has nothing to do with you. Or as a book title says: *What You Think of Me Is None of My Business!*

***

Making Your Intention Your Reality

Here are ten ways to practice nurturing your intention to respect yourself at all times:

1. Look into a mirror, make eye connection with yourself, and say 'I love me' as many times as possible during your day

I love me: These three magic words help you maintain your self-respect. Now, be aware that saying these words may be difficult at first because of the conditions you've been exposed to over a lifetime, and because the words may bring to the surface remnants of disrespect that your ego wants you to hold on to.

Your immediate impulse might be to see this as an expression of your ego's desire to be superior to everyone else. But this is not an ego statement at all – it's an affirmation of self-respect. Transcend that ego mind and affirm your love for yourself and your connection to the Spirit of God. This doesn't make you superior to anyone; it makes you equal to all and celebrates that you're a piece of God. Affirm it for your own self-respect. Affirm it in order to be respectful of that which intended you here. Affirm it because it's the way you'll stay connected to your Source and regain the power of intention. I love me. Say it without embarrassment. Say it proudly, and be that image of love and self-respect.

2. Write the following affirmation and repeat it over and over again to yourself

I am whole and perfect as I was created! Carry this thought with you wherever you go. Have it laminated, and place it in your pocket, on your dashboard, on your refrigerator, or next to your bed – allow the words to become a source of high energy and self-respect. By simply carrying these words with you and being in the same space with them, their energy will flow directly to you.

Self-respect emerges from the fact that you respect the Source from which you came and you've made a decision to reconnect to that Source, regardless of what anyone else might think. It's very important to keep reminding yourself at the beginning that you're worthy of infinite respect from the one Source you can always count on, the piece of God energy that defines you. This reminder will do wonders for your self-respect, and consequently your ability to use the power of intention in your life. Over and over, remind yourself: *I'm not my body. I'm not my accumulations. I'm not my achievements. I'm not my reputation. I am whole and perfect as I was created!*

3. Extend more respect to others and to all of life

Perhaps the greatest secret of self-esteem is to appreciate other people more. The easiest way to do this is to see the unfolding of God in them. Look past the judgements of others' appearance, failures, and successes, their status in society, their wealth or lack of it . . . and extend appreciation and love to the Source from which they came. Everyone is a child of God – everyone! Try to see this even in those who behave in what appears to be a godless fashion. Know that by extending love and respect, you can turn that energy around so that it's heading back to its Source rather than away from it. In short, send out respect because that is what you have to give away. Send out judgement and low energy and that is what you'll attract back. Remember, when you judge another, you do not define them, you define yourself as someone who needs to judge. The same applies to judgements directed at you.

4. Affirm to yourself and all others that you meet, I belong!

A sense of belonging is one of the highest attributes on Abraham Maslow's pyramid of self-actualization. Feeling that you don't belong or you're in the wrong place can be due to a lack of self-respect. Respect yourself and your divinity by knowing that everyone belongs. This should never come into question. Your presence here in the universe is proof alone that you belong here. No person decides if you belong here. No government determines if some belong and some don't. This is an intelligent system that you're a part of. The wisdom of Creation intended you to be here, in this place, in this family with these siblings and parents, occupying this precious space. Say it to yourself and affirm it whenever necessary: *I belong!* And so does everyone else. No one is here by accident!

5. *Remind yourself that you're never alone*

My self-respect stays intact as long as I know that it's impossible for me to be alone. I have a *'senior partner'* who's never abandoned me and who's stuck with me even in moments when I had seemingly deserted my Source. I feel that if the universal mind has enough respect to allow me to come here and to work through me – and to protect me in times when I strayed onto dangerous nonspiritual turf – then this partnership deserves my reciprocal respect. I recall my friend Pat McMahon, a talk-show host on KTAR radio in Phoenix, Arizona, telling me about his encounter with Mother Teresa in his studio before interviewing her for his programme. He pleaded with her to allow him to do something for her: 'Anything at all,' he begged. 'I'd just like to help you in some way.' She looked at him and said: 'Tomorrow morning get up at 4 A.M. and go out onto the streets of Phoenix. Find someone who lives there and believes that he's alone, and convince him that he's not.' Great advice, because everyone who wallows in self-doubt or appears to be lost . . . has lost their self-respect because they've forgotten that they're not alone.

6. *Respect your body!*

You've been provided with a perfect body to house your inner invisible being for a few brief moments in eternity. Regardless of its size, shape, colour, or any imagined infirmities, it's a perfect creation for the purpose that you were intended here for. You don't need to work at getting healthy; health is something you already have if you don't disturb it. You may have disturbed your healthy body by overfeeding it, underexercising it, and overstimulating it with toxins or drugs that make it sick, fatigued, jumpy, anxious, depressed, bloated, ornery, or an endless list of maladies. You can begin the fulfillment of this intention to live a life of self-respect by honoring the temple that houses you. You know what to do. You don't need another diet, workout manual, or personal trainer. Go within, listen to your body, and treat it with all of the dignity and love that your self-respect demands.

7. Meditate to stay in conscious contact with your Source, which always respects you

I can't say this enough: Meditation is a way to experience what the five senses can't detect. When you're connected to the field of intention, you're connected to the wisdom that's within you. That divine wisdom has great respect for you, and it cherishes you while you're here. Meditation is a way to ensure that you stay in a state of self-respect. Regardless of all that goes on around you, when you enter into that sacred space of meditation, all doubts about your value as an esteemed creation dissolve. You'll emerge from the solemnity of meditation feeling connected to your Source and enjoying respect for all beings, particularly yourself.

8. Make amends with adversaries

The act of making amends sends out a signal of respect for your adversaries. By radiating this forgiving energy outward, you'll find this same kind of respectful positive energy flowing back toward you. By being big enough to make amends and replace the energy of anger, bitterness, and tension with kindness – even if you still insist that you're right – you'll respect yourself much more than prior to your act of forgiveness. If you're filled with rage towards anyone, there's a huge part of you that resents the presence of this debilitating energy. Take a moment right here and now to simply face that person who stands out in your mind as someone you hurt, or directed hurt to you, and tell him or her that you'd like to make amends. You'll notice how much better you feel. That good feeling of having cleared the air is self-respect. It takes much more courage, strength of character, and inner conviction to make amends than it does to hang on to the low-energy feelings.

9. Always remember the self in self-respect

In order to do this, you must recognize that the opinions of others toward you aren't facts, they're opinions. When I speak to an audience of 500 people, there are 500 opinions of me in the room at the end of the evening. I'm none of those opinions. I can't be responsible for how they view me. The only thing I can be responsible for is my own character, and this is true for every one of us. If I respect myself, then I'm relying on the *self* in self-respect. If I doubt myself, or punish myself, I've not only lost my self-respect, I'll continue to attract more and more doubt and lower-energy opinions with which to further punish myself. You can't stay linked to the universal mind, which intends all of us here, if you fail to rely on your self for your self-respect.

10. Be in a state of gratitude.

You'll discover that gratitude is the final step in each succeeding chapter. Be an appreciator rather than a depreciator of everything that shows up in your life. When you're saying *Thank you, God, for everything*, and when you're expressing gratitude for your life and all that you see and experience, you're respecting Creation. This respect is within you, and you can only give away what you have inside. Being in a state of gratitude is the same thing as being in a state of respect – respect for yourself, which you give away freely, and which will return to you tenfold.

***

Finally, I come to some simple keys which are rather important for you to create Happiness in your life.

JOY

A hectic schedule crammed with non-purposeful

activities precludes an experience of inspiration. For example, when we accept obligatory committee assignments or board appointments, requests to write on subjects that don't inspire us, or invitations to gatherings we don't want to attend, we feel joy draining from our body and spirit.

Our life must be open to Spirit's guidance in order for us to feel inspired. When the calendar becomes frenzied, full of unnecessary turbulence because we've failed to simplify, we won't be able to hear those long-distance calls from our Source . . . and we'll slip into stress, anguish, and even depression. So whatever it takes to feel joy, we simply must act upon it.

Regardless of our current station in life, we have a spiritual contract to make joy our constant companion – so we must learn to make a conscious choice to say no to anything that takes us away from an inspired life. This can be done gently, while clearly showing others that this is how we choose to live. We can start by turning down requests that involve actions that don't correspond with our inner knowing about why we're here.

Even at work, we can find ways to keep ourselves on an inspirational agenda. For example, during my years as a college professor, I recall being asked over and over to partake in activities that didn't correspond with my own inspiration. So I devised a simple solution: I took on more teaching assignments, and in exchange, my colleagues attended curriculum meetings, served on research committees, and wrote building-improvement reports. I consistently listened to my heart, which always demanded joy.

Keep in mind that it's only difficult or impossible to accomplish joy when we engage in resistant vibrational thinking. If we know that we don't have to live a life stuffed with non-joyful activities, then we can choose the way of inspiration. Opting for joy involves giving ourselves time for play instead of scheduling a workaholic nightmare. *We deserve to feel joy – it's our spiritual calling*. By giving ourselves free time to read, meditate, exercise, and walk in nature, we're inviting the guidance that's waiting patiently to come calling with inspirational messages.

There's also no law requiring us to be at the continual beck and call of our family members. I see no reason to feel anything but joy when we know it's right to choose to do what we're called to do, even when it interferes with another family member's calling. In fact, children benefit by knowing that the business of parenting is to teach them how *not* to lean on their parents. Raising independent kids to find their own inspiration and look for their own joy is important for everyone – we want them to be doing what they're called to do, ultimately for themselves, not for us. We can take great joy in attending their soccer games and recitals and in being with them and their friends – and when we're inspired, we actually *enjoy* their activities. But let's help them to live their joy, and be able to do it with or *without* us there to cheer them on.

The bottom line is that we can simplify life by cutting down on the busywork that keeps us off purpose. We must curtail such activities and listen to Spirit, staying aware of joy and how simple it is to access.

LOVE

Thoughts or actions that aren't tuned to love will prevent inspiration from getting through to us – we need to remember that we come from a Source of pure love, so a simple life means incorporating that love as one of the three mainstays of our material existence.

This little four-line poem from the *Rubaiyat of Omar Khayyam*, written approximately 1,000 years ago, says so much about staying focused on love:

> Ah, love! could thou and I with fate conspire
> To grasp this sorry scheme of things entire,
> Would not we shatter it to bits – and then
> Re-mould it nearer to the heart's desire!

On the fateful day of 11 September 2001, what stuck in my mind were the cell-phone calls made by the people on the ill-fated planes. Every single call was made to a loved one, to connect back in love or to express final words of love. No one called the office or asked their stockbroker for a final appraisal of their financial status, as relationships that weren't love based didn't enter the thoughts of those who knew they were leaving this physical world. Their top priority was to be certain to close out their lives in love: 'Tell the kids that I love them.' 'I love you!' 'Give Mom and Dad my love.'

Just as love is the priority in the final moments of life, so it must be as we simplify life *now*. We can go toward a clearer life by examining and purifying our relationships with those we love, with ourselves, and with God. What we're looking for are connections that keep us in an energy of love, which is the highest and fastest energy in the Universe. Love is also incredibly healing, which reminds me of an article I recently read. Called 'The Rescuing Hug,' it detailed the first week in the life of a set of twins, one of whom wasn't expected to live. The babies were in two separate incubators, but nurse Gayle Kasparian fought hospital rules to place them together in one. When Gayle did so, the healthier of the twins threw an arm over her sister in an endearing embrace – at which point, the weaker baby's heart rate stabilized and her temperature rose to normal.

Even as tiny infants, our spiritually based instincts tell us to love one another. It's such a simple message, yet it's so powerful. If we organize our life around love – for God, for ourselves, for family and friends, for all humankind, and for the environment – we'll remove a lot of the chaos and disorder that defines our life. This is a way to simplify our life, but more than that, it's a way to attract inspiration.

PEACE

Isn't our all-time highest priority to live in peace? We come from a place of peace, yet we've somehow gotten farther and farther away from these origins. When we hooked up with ego, we opted for chaos, even though peace was right there for us. And inspiration and being peaceful go hand in hand.

I know that having inner and outer peace is simply crucial for me. I eschew turmoil, conflict, and agitation and remove myself from these noninspiring elements at every opportunity. After all, I can't be the spiritual being I desire to be or live in God-realization when I'm engaged in any form of bedlam.

Many people who have a semi-celebrity status as myself are surrounded by a long list of people who orchestrate virtually every aspect of their lives. I, however, have chosen a simpler route, and the Universe has responded by sending me a very few individuals who've supported my desire for peace. I'd like to spend the rest of this section discussing each one of them so that you'll have some clear illustrations of how these wonderful people have helped me stay in-Spirit.

— Years ago I realized that I needed help in managing the affairs of my growing enterprise, yet the idea of agents, business managers, advisors, attorneys, accountants, mediators, personal trainers, bodyguards, and any number of people to represent me seemed beyond my tolerance level. Many of those who do what I do even on a smaller scale have a large entourage of attendants for all manner of duties and activities. And I've had these contemporaries complain to me about being burdened with all of their representatives and spending more than they take in to support the services of all these individuals.

This is not my way – in fact, I have *one person* who handles almost all of my requirements. One day while running a training session for a marathon, God sent me the perfect person to handle so many of my upcoming unforeseen pressures and requirements, in the form of a woman who'd left high school in a foreign country to come to America with her two daughters. She doesn't have any fancy degrees or specialized skills, but what she does have is a heart as big as the sky, fierce loyalty, and a willingness to do whatever it takes to learn with on-the-job training.

Originally from Finland (but now a U.S. citizen), Maya Labos is the ultimate definition of a multitasker. In three decades, she's never said: 'I can't do that; it's not my job.' She manages every request, answers my mail, books all of my talks and my appearances with the media, takes me to and from airports, maintains my personal privacy by deflecting low-energy requests, and deals with the hundreds of appeals I get for endorsements and writing requests. Yet she also handles innumerable tasks, including grocery shopping, vitamin purchasing, office tidying, or bringing clothes to the cleaners – I can count on her to take care of everything and anything I need.

When I met Maya almost 30 years ago, she was completely broke; today she owns her own home by the ocean and is my best friend, confidante, and associate. You see, when we're open to matching up our desire for peace and simplicity with the peace and simplicity from which we originated, God sends what we need. In my case, I got an 'entourage of one' to handle what myriad 'specialists' can't do for so many of my contemporaries.

— Every writer needs an editor. Almost 30 years ago, God saw this and sent one to me in the form of the enormously well-read and competent Joanna Pyle. She's been my one and only editorial person for the 25 plus books I've written; I don't submit to editorial boards. Joanna does for me what many writers ask for from their team of editors, editorial assistants, line editors, rewriters, revisers, amenders, annotators, and so on. I want to keep it simple, and Joanna knows how I write. She's also the only person who can read my scribbles, since I write in longhand.

As the computer age dawned on the publishing world, Joanna trained herself to meet these newly emerging technological requirements – she didn't ask me to write on a computer or to change anything. She knows my desire for simplicity and peace, and she accommodates me perfectly. When I finish a chapter, I send it to Joanna with complete trust that she'll edit it in such a manner that it will be consistent with my original intent. She transcribes it, types it, reorganizes it, and computerizes it – all with a smile and genuine gratitude for being able to fulfill her purpose. Joanna is me; I am Joanna.

Once I was able to convince her to leave her non-fulfilling employment as a flight attendant and pursue her bliss as an editor full-time, she was finally able to feel the joy and peace that comes from matching up her energy with her desires. She lives inspiration, and she allows me to do the same.

— I only employ one individual who handles any and all matters related to the complexities of taxes, particularly where foreign royalties are concerned. I don't use a team of legal experts who charge by the hour, or tax consultants who receive as much as what I owe the government. One man, Bob Adelson, knows my desire for peace by keeping it simple, so he organizes everything for me. He works diligently and thoroughly, doing what he loves, and I treasure his presence in my life.

— In 1976, after *Your Erroneous Zones* was published, I decided to move from New York to Florida. I knew absolutely no one in my new hometown, yet I needed an investment person whom I could trust to help me with the bonuses I'd received from the success of my first book. Having been a teacher and university professor before this point, with no experience in (or money for) investing, I knew practically nothing about this world. While contemplating how to start an investment portfolio, I pulled into a gas station, filled my tank, and drove away without realizing that my wallet, which contained $800 in cash, had fallen out of the car and was lying next to the pump.

Just a few hours later, a man called to tell me that he'd found my wallet – including the cash. I went to meet John Darling, who was my angel sent from God to take care of all of my investments for the next 29 years (and he continues to be one of my very best friends and confidants). When I needed someone I could trust, the Universe sent me a stranger who returned my $800... and I've never had a moment of nonpeace regarding investments in the past three decades. John has managed it all for me – always keeping in mind how I like things to be simple, risk free, and uncomplicated – knowing what my ultimate investment objectives were and what I desired for my family.

— I left a large, prestigious New York publishing firm to work with Hay House, mainly because everything in the Big Apple was becoming way too complex. My former publisher employed wonderful people, but the company was too big – it had too many tentacles, too many unkept promises, and too many departments that weren't in harmony with each other (or with me). I felt that too often I was being told, 'It's not our fault. The fault is over there in finance or over there in marketing or over there in distribution.' It was like a 20-headed monster.

I voted once again for tranquility and simplicity, and once again God sent me a gift – this time in the form of the president and CEO of Louise Hay's publishing company, Hay House. When I met Reid Tracy, we clicked almost immediately. This man – who's unafraid to roll up his sleeves and unload trucks, even though he's in an executive position – promised me personal attention, and he delivered. We talked every day about a publishing company that didn't get so big that it forgot to care for its authors. Reid promised me no large conglomerates and said: 'If you have a desire, make it known to me, and I'll act on it.' I loved the lack of complications, since I didn't wish to be in a large-business labyrinth any longer. *Simplify, simplify, simplify!*

It has been a glorious experience for both Reid (whom I now consider one of my closest friends) and myself. I wanted peace as a writer, and Louise Hay, whom I've long admired, and her fine president have allowed me to create in peace.

As you can see, I've chosen to allow the world of Spirit to send me those individuals who have helped, rather than hindered, me. Without these fine people and their treasured friendship, I wouldn't be able to be here in Maui, playing tennis and walking on the beach. But mostly I'm able to write from my heart and do it in peaceful ease, knowing that the Universe has taken care of all the details in its own Divine way. When *you* desire peace, simplicity, and honesty and send out a matching vibration to those desires, all I can say is, 'Start watching. It's on its way!'

The 12-Step Programme to Simplicity

In fine, I'm going to give you 12 very specific tools for simplifying your life. Begin using them today if you're serious about hearing that ultimate call to inspiration, for creating Happiness in your life.

1. Unclutter your life

You'll feel a real rush of inspiration when you clear out stuff that's no longer useful in your life:

> If you haven't worn it in the past year or two, recycle it for others to use.
> Get rid of old files that take up space and are seldom, if ever, needed.
> Donate unused toys, tools, books, bicycles, and dishes to a charitable organization.

Get rid of anything that keeps you mired in acquisitions that contribute to a cluttered life. In the words of Socrates, 'He is nearest to God who needs the fewest things.' So the less you need to insure, protect, dust, reorganize, and move, the closer you'll be to hearing inspiration's call.

2. Clear your calendar of unwanted and unnecessary activities and obligations

If you're unavailable for Spirit, you're unlikely to know the glow of inspiration. Had I not been free enough to go running each day back in the 1970s, no Maya. Had I not moved away from the frenetic rush of New York to Florida (where I longed to be), no John. Had I spent all my time on a demanding board, no Joanna. God will indeed work with you and send you the guidance – and the people – you need, but if you're grossly overscheduled, you're going to miss these life-altering gifts. So practice saying no to excessive demands and don't feel guilty about injecting a dose of leisure time into your daily routine.

3. Be sure to keep your free time free

Be on the lookout for invitations to functions that may keep you on top of society's pyramid, but that inhibit your access to joyful inspiration. If cocktail parties, social get-togethers, fund-raising events, or even drinking-and-gossiping gatherings with friends aren't really how you want to spend your free time, then don't. Begin declining invitations that don't activate feelings of inspiration.

I find that an evening spent reading or writing letters, watching a movie with a loved one, having dinner with my children, or even exercising alone is far more inspiring than getting dressed to attend a function often filled with small talk. I've learned to be unavailable for such events without apologizing, and consequently have more inspired moments freed up.

4. *Take time for meditation and yoga*

Give yourself at least 20 minutes a day to sit quietly and make conscious contact with God. I've written an entire book on this subject called *Getting in the Gap*, so I won't belabour it here. I will say that I've received thousands of messages from people all over the world, who have expressed their appreciation for learning how to simplify their life by taking the time to meditate.

I also encourage you to find a yoga center near you and begin a regular practice. The rewards are so powerful: You'll feel healthier, less stressed, and inspired by what you'll be able to do with and for your body in a very short time.

5. *Return to the simplicity of nature*

There's nothing more awe inspiring than nature itself. The fantasy to return to a less tumultuous life almost always involves living in the splendor of the mountains, the forests, or the tundra; on an island; near the ocean; or beside a lake. These are universal urges, since nature is created by the same Source as we are, and we're made up of the same chemicals as all of nature (we're stardust, remember?).

Your urge to simplify and feel inspired is fueled by the desire to be your natural self – that is, your *nature* self.

So give yourself permission to get away to trek or camp in the woods; swim in a river, lake, or ocean; sit by an open fire; ride horseback through trails; or ski down a mountain slope. This doesn't have to mean long, planned vacations that are months away – no matter where you live, you're only a few hours or even moments away from a park, campground, or trail that will allow you to enjoy a feeling of being connected to the entire Universe.

6. Put distance between you and your critics

Choose to align yourself with people who are like-minded in their search for simplified inspiration. Give those who find fault or who are confrontational a silent blessing and remove yourself from their energy as quickly as possible. Your life is simplified enormously when you don't have to defend yourself to anyone, and when you receive support rather than criticism. You don't have to endure the criticism with anything other than a polite thank-you and a promise to consider what's been said – anything else is a state of conflict that erases the possibility of your feeling inspired. You never need to defend yourself or your desires to anyone, as those inner feelings are Spirit speaking to you. Those thoughts are sacred, so don't ever let anyone trample on them.

7. Take some time for your health

Consider that the number one health problem in America, as in many other countries, seems to be obesity.

How can you feel inspired and live in simplicity if you're gorging on excessive amounts of food and eliminating the exercise that the body craves? Recall that your body is a sacred temple where you reside for this lifetime, so make some time every single day for exercising it. Even if you can only manage a walk around the block, just do it. Similarly, keep the words *portion control* uppermost in your consciousness – your stomach is the size of your fist, not a wheelbarrow! Respect your sacred temple *and* simplify your life by being an exerciser and a sensible eater. I promise that you'll feel inspired if you act on this today!

8. *Play, play, play!*

You'll simplify your life and feel inspired if you learn to play rather than work your way through life. I love to be around kids because they inspire me with their laughter and frivolity. In fact, if I've heard it once, I've heard it a thousand times: 'Wayne, you've never grown up – you're always playing.' I take great pride in this! I play onstage when I speak, and I'm playing now as I write.

Many years ago I was given a tremendous opportunity to appear on *The Tonight Show* with Johnny Carson. The man who took a chance on me, booking me even though I was an unknown at the time, was a talent coordinator named Howard Papush. It was my first big break, and I went on to appear on that show 36 additional times.

Now it's my turn to say thank you to Howard. He's written a wonderful book titled *When's Recess? Playing Your Way Through the Stresses of Life*, which I encourage you to read. (Howard also conducts workshops that teach people how to play and have fun in life.) In the book, Howard shares this great quote from Richard Bach: 'You are led through your lifetime by the inner learning creature, the playful spiritual being that is your real self.' I couldn't agree more – by all means, get back in touch with your real, playful self, and take every opportunity to play! Notice how it makes everything so sweet, and so simple.

9. Slow down

One of Mahatma Gandhi's most illuminating observations reminds us that 'there is more to life than increasing its speed.' This is great advice for simplifying your life – in fact, slow everything way down for a few moments right here and now. Slowly read these words. Slow your breathing down so that you're aware of each inhalation and exhalation. . . .

When you're in your car, downshift and relax. Slow down your speech, your inner thoughts, and the frantic pace of everything you do. Take more time to hear others. Notice your inclination to interrupt and get the conversation over with, and then choose to listen instead. Stop to enjoy the stars on a clear night and the cloud formations on a crisp day. Sit down in a mall and just observe how everyone seems in a hurry to get nowhere.

By slowing down, you'll simplify and rejoin the perfect pace at which creation works. Imagine trying to hurry nature up by tugging at an emerging tomato plant – you're as natural as that plant, so let yourself be at peace with the perfection of nature's plan.

10. Do everything you can to eschew debt

Remember that you're attempting to simplify your life here, so you don't need to purchase more of what will complicate and clutter your life. If you can't afford it, let it go until you can. By going into debt, you'll just add layers of anxiety onto your life. That anxiety will then take you away from your peace, which is where you are when you're in-Spirit. When you have to work extra hard to pay off debts, the present moments of your life are less enjoyable; consequently, you're further away from the joy and peace that are the trademarks of inspiration. You're far better off to have less and enjoy the days of your life than to take on debt and invite stress and anxiety where peace and tranquility could have reigned. And remember that the money you have in your possession is nothing but energy – so refuse to plug in to an energy system that's not even there.

11. Forget about the cash value

I try not to think about money too frequently because it's been my observation that people who do so tend to think about almost nothing else. So do what your heart tells you will bring you joy, rather than determining whether it will be cost-effective. If you'd really enjoy that whale-watching trip, for instance, make the decision to do so – don't deny yourself the pleasures of life because of some monetary detail. Don't base your purchases on getting a discount, and don't rob yourself of a simple joy because you didn't get a break on the price. You can afford a happy, fulfilling life, and if you're busy right now thinking that I have some nerve telling you this because of your bleak financial picture, then you have your own barrier of resistance.

Make an attempt to free yourself from placing a price tag on everything you have and do – after all, in the world of Spirit, there are no price tags. Don't make money the guiding principle for what you have or do; rather, simplify your life and return to Spirit by finding the inherent value in everything. A dollar does not determine worth, even though you live in a world that attempts to convince you otherwise.

12. Remember your spirit

When life tends to get too complex, too fast, too cluttered, too deadline oriented, or too type A for you, stop and remember your own spirit. You're headed for inspiration, a simple, peaceful place where you're in harmony with the perfect timing of all creation. Go there in your mind, and stop frequently to remember what you really want.

***

I will leave you with a quote from Albert Einstein: 'Possessions, outward success, publicity, luxury – to me these have always been contemptible. I believe that a simple and unassuming manner of life is best for everyone, best both for the body and the mind.'

Wow! I'd say this is pretty good advice, wouldn't you?

Contributors

His Holiness the **14th Dalai Lama**, Tenzin Gyatso, is the spiritual leader of Tibet. He was born on 6 July 1935, in northeastern Tibet and was recognized two years later as the reincarnation of of Thubten Gyatso, the 13th Dalai Lama. He travels extensively – having visited more than 62 countries – giving speeches to promote understanding, kindness,compassion, respect for the environment, and above all, world peace. In 1989, he was awarded the Nobel Peace Prize for his nonviolent struggle for the liberation of Tibet. He lives in Mcleaodganj, Dharamsala, India.

Deepak Chopra, one of the world's greatest leaders in the field of mind-body medicine, is the author of over seventy books, which have been translated into thirty-five languages. Hailed by *Time* magazine as 'the poet-prophet of alternative medecine', he is the founder of the Chopra Center for Well Being in La Jolla, California.

His Holiness the 17th Gyalwang **Karmapa** is one of Tibetan Buddhism's most senior lamas. Born in 1985 in a nomad family in eastern Tibet, he was discovered to be the seventeenth Karmapa, Ogyen Drodul Trinley Dorje in 1992. Head of the Karma Kagyu, one of the major Tibetan Buddhist schools, the Karmapas are Tibet's great wisdom teachers, and the oldest lineage of Buddhism. Since his dramatic escape to India in 1999, he has been residing at the Gyuto Tantric Monastery, near Dharamsala, India.

Born in 1954 in eastern Tibet, the **12th Chamgon Kenting Tai Situpa** (Pema Donyo Nyinje) was formally recognized and enthroned at the age of 18 months, by the 16th Gyalwang Karmapa, as the twelfth in line of the successive incarnations of the Tai Situpas. A renowned Buddhist teacher and scholar, a poet, calligrapher, artist he has authored several books on Buddhism and arts. At the 22, he assumed his historic responsibility and founded the Palpung Sherabling monastic seat near Baijnath, Himachal Pradesh, India where he lives.

Going on 98, **Khushwant Singh** is one of India's best-known writers and columnists. Author of classics such as *Train to Pakistan*, *I Shall Not Hear the Nightingale* and *Delhi* his non-fiction includes the classic two-volume *A History of the Sikhs* and a number of translations and works on Sikh religion and culture, nature, current affairs and Urdu poetry. His autobiography *Truth, Love and a Little Malice* was published in 2002. He was awarded the Padma Bhushan in 1974, the Punjab Rattan in 2006 and the Padma Vibhushan, the country's second highest civilian award, in 2007. He lives in New Delhi.

Robert Holden, Ph.D, is the Director of The Happiness Project and Success Intelligence. -- two pioneering projects that work closely with leaders in business, health care, education and politics. His innovative work on happiness and success has been featured on Oprah and in two major BBC-TV documentaries. His *The Happiness Formula* and *How to Be Happy*, has been shown in 16 countries to more than 30 million television viewers. He is the author of ten bestselling books.

Rohini Singh has done different things at different times in her life. Author of eight bestselling cookbooks published in the US, the UK and India, and two novels for children, today she practices a number of healing therapies including reiki, refloxology, hypnotherapy, emotional freedom techniques and theta healing, and conducts regular personal growth workshops and healing retreats both in India and overseas. She lives in Gurgaon, near Delhi.

Shobhaa **D**é is one of India's highest selling authors and a popular social commentator. Her works comprising both fiction and non-fiction have been featured in comparative literature courses at universities abroad and in India. Her writing has been translated into many regional languages as well as French, German, Hungarian, Italian, Korean, Portuguese, Russian, Spanish and Turkish. She lives in Mumbai.

Born in 1956, **Sri Sri Ravi Shankar** is the founder of The Art of Living Foundation, a humanitarian organization that is represented in over 150 countries worldwide. It also instructs people in spiritual stress management. As an ambassador of peace he communicates his vision of a world free of stress and violence at international forums and global meetings. He lives outside Bangalore, India.

Wayne **W. Dyer**, Ph.D., is an internationally renowned author and speaker in the field of self-development. Author of 90 books, he has created many audio programmes and videos, and has appeared on thousands of television and radio shows. He holds a doctorate in educational counseling from Wayne State University and was an associate professor at St. John's University in New York.